Prayer

Prayer

DUDLEY WRIGHT

INTRODUCTION BY
ALLAN ARMSTRONG

FOREWORD BY
JAMES L. MACBETH BAIN

IBIS PRESS
An Imprint of Nicolas-Hays, Inc.
Berwick, Maine

Published in 2004 by Ibis Press
An imprint of Nicolas-Hays, Inc.
P. O. Box 1126
Berwick, ME 03901-1126
www.nicolashays.com

Distributed to the trade by
Red Wheel/Weiser, LLC
P. O. Box 612
York Beach, ME 03910-0612
www.redwheelweiser.com

Foreword copyright © 2004 Allan Armstrong

Library of Congress Cataloging-in-Publication Data
available on request.

Cover design by Kathryn Sky-Peck.
Text design by Studio 31
Typeset in Adobe Sabon 12/16
Printed in the United States of America

10   09   08   07   06   05   04
7   6   5   4   3   2   1

Say what is prayer when it is prayer indeed?
The mighty utterance of a mighty need.
The man is praying, who doth press with might
Out of his darkness into God's own light.

R. C. Trench

CONTENTS

FOREWORD

OW GREAT IS THE POWER OF PRAYER! Who of us can esteem it aright? Who can say where its efficacy ends? Surely it is the great power that we human spirits can wield—great because it only works in the way of blessing. For it is only a power of Good. Not otherwise may it come into operation.

This is the Prayer of which our writer here discourses so fluently and ably.

And so it gives me an intense pleasure to say now that I have read this treatise with great satisfaction and true benefit. Indeed, it has been a real refreshing to read it through. And so much have I enjoyed it that for the most part I have read it over and over again. Did I only cull the one thought from its perusal as expressed in p. 100, where the petition "Give us this day our daily bread" is said to be translated by more than one as "May we remain content with our daily lot," I were well repaid for the effort of reading. But such suggestive thoughts are many and are most chastely expressed throughout. Clear in thought and yet rich in feeling is this word—truly a catholic word on a great Catholic theme.

And the sooner we come to this true catholicity in our religious thought the better. For then we are neither Roman nor Greek nor Buddhist nor Mohammedan, but all these, and more than these, in Christ. In Christ we are whole in doctrine, catholic in sentiment, sane in judgment, ever blessed in all we do. I do trust that this treatise may find its way to the hands of the many truly spiritual mystics to whom it would indeed be as a feast of fat things.

James L. Macbeth Bain

INTRODUCTION

hen I first read this book on prayer, I was moved by its simple yet profound message. Dudley Wright's inspiring and thought-provoking ideas led me into rich avenues of meditation wherein I reflected upon both its ancient lineage and significance in the world today. In times past, it was generally accepted that prayer enshrined the noblest thoughts, aspirations, concepts, and ideals of humankind. During the course of these meditations, a question emerged that initially appeared to be simple enough, but on further investigation proved difficult to answer in a way that is both objective and meaningful. The question is simply, "What is prayer?" That Dudley Wright does not provide a definitive answer to this question is not surprising as he wrote from a standpoint that assumed his readers, living in an essentially religious society, had some understanding of what prayer actually meant. He wrote within a social context that had many levels of interpretation built into it over the course of countless generations. The spiritual ethos that sustained prayer had never really been disturbed by the political changes in religion, thus it had never been called upon to justify or define itself, for it was always a part of the fabric of the social order. However, the same cannot be said of society today. Dudley Wright's world more or less ended with the outbreak of war in 1939, and out of its ashes emerged a new order whose immediate appetite was perceived to be, and indeed still is, fundamentally material.

This appetite, once unfettered, gave rise to an unprecedented growth in world consumerism, which, along with related developments in science and technology, effected a major change in the intellectual life of civilization. Society has subsequently become permeated with a materialistic philosophy that often assumes the name of Humanism but in fact is an extreme form of Materialism[1] that has not only rejected, but is hostile to religion, the spiritual life, and all spiritual thinking; a philosophical stance that is radically different from that of Renaissance luminaries such as Erasmus, Thomas More, and Ficino, who along with other spiritually-minded thinkers founded the great intellectual movement known as Humanism.

Humanism began in Renaissance Italy during the early part of the 15th century. Its originators sought to revive the study of classical Greco-Roman thought, embodied in ancient texts that had been lost to the major part of the Western world for centuries. The movement was called "Humanism" because it provided a basis for an education in *humanitas* (better known today as the humanities). Its philosophical focus was the intrinsic worth of Man, emphasizing human welfare and the fulfillment of human interests in this life without undue reference to the transcendental or spiritual world. The main exponents of Renaissance Humanism were concerned with promoting religious and social tolerance. One of the chief advocates, Desiderius Erasmus,[2] campaigned for many years for peaceful reform in the undivided Church, rather than the internecine conflicts that came with the Reformation. Another, Sir Thomas More,[3] revealed to the world in his *Utopia* a model society based on the natural reasoning power of humanity without spiritual revelation, while Ficino,[4] protégé of Cosimo Medici and head of the New Academy of Florence, translated for the first time the complete works of Plato into Latin as well as various other works on Neoplatonism.

It should not be forgotten that Humanism was a movement conceived within Christianity by Christians and nurtured by Christians such as Ficino, Nicholas of Cusa, John Colet, and Pico della Mirandola. It was also championed by popes Nicholas V, Pius II, and Leo X. Today, those who call themselves humanists are almost all agnostics, materialists, or avowed atheists. It should also be noted that Materialism has long been a part of the human intellectual landscape. Indeed one of the most notable of the early exponents of Materialism was the Greek philosopher Leucippus,[5] who, along with his student Democritus,[6] is credited with being the originator of the theory of Atomism, an essentially materialistic description of the universe. However, the more modern cult of materialism, which emerged during the late 17th century, much influenced by the writings of Thomas Hobbes,[7] is far more extreme than the philosophy of Leucippus and Democritus in its denial of the existence of God, of the soul, and of the continuity of life after death, promoting instead the pessimistic viewpoint that human life along with all of its beliefs, aspirations, and loves is nothing more than the result of the random combining of atoms, and ceases at the moment of death, thus reducing our cultural perception of consciousness to a temporary biological function.

By claiming the credit for being the philosophy underlying the amazing scientific and technological developments of the 19th and 20th centuries, the proponents of Materialism have in the name of Humanism dominated the intellectual landscape of our culture, resulting in the dismantling of religion and the secularization of society. As a result, the word "prayer" now reveals less and less of its meaning in modern everyday language and is becoming increasingly difficult to explain objectively. Thus the question, "What is prayer?" is a question that is probably more pertinent now than at any other time in our history. But how is it to be answered? Are we to view prayer as the last hope of the desperate as argued by the proponents of materialism, whose philosophy provides little more than the cold comfort of a

grim and meaningless existence, or, are we to
view prayer in spiritual terms and accept it as
a means by which we can elevate our hearts
and our minds to fellowship with God, and in
communion therewith receive inspiration and
develop a greater understanding of our world?

If we accept prayer in the latter, positive
sense, it necessarily follows that we accept God
as a conscious living being, because the essence
of prayer is "communing with God"; and
although a full discussion on the nature of God
is outside the scope of the present work, we
may accept, with some degree of certainty, that
humanity's definition of God as the source,
ground, and destiny of being embodies the
totality of purpose and meaning of human
existence in a framework of absolute consciousness, and it is only in this context that
prayer can be defined in an objective and meaningful way. However, this is conceptually far
removed from our general understanding.
Indeed, for most of us, our understanding of
prayer rarely transcends the notion of pleading
or asking for a special favor from a divine
source, which in itself is interesting as the ety-
mological root of the word "prayer" is derived

from the Latin *prex*, which means an entreaty
or request, particularly from a god. Be that as it
may, no matter how accurate this definition
may be, it is insufficient to describe the vital
part that prayer plays in the soul's intimate
relationship with God, which is far more than
begging or plea-bargaining with divinity. It is
an act of friendship, of love, of personally sharing with the source and destiny of our being
what we can never share with another person.
It is communication at the most intimate and
essential level, a communication initiated by
the soul and reciprocated by God.

It is then not surprising that from the earliest times prayer has been central to the life of
humanity, indeed, many of the earliest records
we have are prayers or hymns to the divine. The
people of ancient Egypt may well have been
pragmatic but they were not philosophical
materialists. To them, life on this earth meant
far more than mere survival; they recognized
that the end of a human life was but a beginning of another superior life. That much is
obvious, even from a casual examination of the
records they left on the walls of the earliest
pyramids. These "Pyramid Texts," as they are

called, date from the 3rd millennium B.C. and
constitute the oldest corpus of religious literature available to us. They contain a vast
amount of information concerning the Egyptian understanding of the spiritual life. Without
doubt many of the prayers of ancient Egypt, as
of any other culture, were prayers of need, or at
least perceived need. As, for example, this
excerpt from a prayer accredited to a certain
Nebensi, a scribe and artist of the Temple of
Ptah:

> [O thou god Hetep]
> . . . Let me gain dominion within the Field,
> for I know it, and I have sailed among its
> lakes so that I might come into its cities. My
> mouth is strong; and I am equipped against
> the khus; let them not have dominion over
> me. Let me be rewarded with thy fields, O
> thou god Hetep; that which is thy wish shalt
> thou do, O lord of the winds. May I become
> a Khu therein, may I eat therein, may I drink
> therein, may I plough therein, may I reap
> therein, may I fight therein, may I make love
> therein, may my words be mighty therein,
> may I never be in a state of servitude therein,
> but may I be in authority therein. . .[8]

Yet they also embodied some of the more sublime human ideas and concepts. The following is attributed to the scribe Mes-em-neter, a servant of the God Amen:

> Hymn of praise to thee O god who makest the moment to advance, thou dweller among mysteries of every kind, thou guardian of the word which I speak. Behold, the god hath shame of me, but let my faults be washed away and let them fall upon both hands of the god of Right and Truth. Do away utterly with the transgression which is in me together with my wickedness and sinfulness, O god of Right and Truth. May this god be at peace with me! Do away utterly with the obstacles which are between thee and me. . . ⁹

The prayers of ancient Egypt span several millennia and enshrine an intimate relationship between the soul of the people and God. For the Egyptian, the spiritual world and the mundane world permeated each other in the perpetual rhythm of life, thus establishing meaning at the very root of human existence, and it seems difficult to imagine today that for thousands of years a whole civilization was grounded in a spiritual ethos that gave certainty to the meaning of existence. Yet Egypt was not alone in its convictions. In the fertile lands of Mesopotamia that lie between the rivers Tigris and Euphrates, civilizations were established one upon another. The ancient culture of Sumer gave way to the founders of Babylon who in due course gave way to the Assyrians. Each one rooted, as Egypt, in a world that had both a mundane and spiritual dimension. In a Sumerian epic the following hymn occurs:

> O lord, in thy city which thou lovest, may thy heart be at rest. In the temple of Nippur, thy city, which thou lovest, may thy heart be at rest. When thou joyfully enterest the temple Shumera, the dwelling place of thy heart's contentment, say to thy wife, the maiden queen of Nippur, What is in thy heart, say to her what is in thy mind, say to her the kindly words of one who is forever king.[10]

Close in spirit to this Sumerian hymn is a prayer addressed to the god Bel by an *Urigalla*, or high priest, on the second day of the Babylonian New Year Festival. It is a plea for the protection and wellbeing of the people of Babel.

Bel, without equal in his anger; Bel, merciful king, lord of the lands,
  Causing the great gods to be favourably disposed; Bel, whose glance overthrows the mighty; Lord of kings, light of mankind, fixer of destinies. Bel, Babel is thy seat, Borsippa is thy crown. The wide heavens compose thy liver; Bel, with thine eyes thou dost behold the universe; With thine oracles thou dost control the oracles; with thy glance thou dost give the law; With thine arms thou dost crush the mighty; thy people thou dost grasp with thine hand; When thou dost see them thou dost take pity on them; thou causest them to see the light; they declare thy might. Lord of the lands, light of the Igigi, who dost bestow blessing; who will not speak of thee? Who will not declare thy might? Who will not tell of thy glory? Who will not praise thy kingdom? Lord of the lands, whose dwelling is in E-ud-ul; who dost take the hand of him who has fallen; have mercy on thy city, Babel! Establish the liberty of the children of Babel, objects of thy protection. . .[11]

In the foregoing prayers it is easy to see that the concerns of the high priest are for the well-being of the people and for the administration of society. In principle they are no different from the prayers of our own generation. The concerns are the same—for peace, prosperity, good government, and the general health and humor of the people and their rulers.

In ancient Israel, the same principal concerns are addressed. The most important scriptural reference point is the Bible, particularly the first five books, known as the Pentateuch and the Torah (Law). They contain divine instruction given by God to the people of Israel about how they should live in the world and how they should order their lives around God. Later books of the Bible contain many prayers and hymns that demonstrate the intimate and dynamic nature of Israel's relationship with God, particularly concerning the Torah. For example, in the first Book of Kings it is written that Solomon stood before the altar of the Lord in the presence of the assembled people of Israel and prayed thus:

> Lord God of Israel, there is no god in heaven above or on earth below like you, who keep

your covenant and mercy with your servants who walk before you with all their hearts. You have kept what you promised your servant David my father; You have both spoken with your mouth and fulfilled it with your hand, as it is this day. Therefore Lord God of Israel, now keep what you promised your servant David my father, saying "You shall not fail to have a man sit before me on the throne of Israel, only if your sons take heed to their way, that they walk before me as you have walked before me." And now I pray, O God of Israel, let your words come true, which you have spoke to your servant David my father. But will God indeed dwell on the earth? Behold, heaven and the heaven of heavens cannot contain you. How much less this temple which I built! Yet regard the prayer of your servant and his supplication, O my Lord my God, and listen to the cry and the prayer which your servant is praying before you today: "that your eyes may be open toward this temple night and day, toward the place which you said 'My name shall be there,' that you may hear the prayer that your servant makes towards this place..."[12]

The prayers of Israel are probably nowhere better enshrined than in the Psalms, many of which are traditionally attributed to King David, the father of Solomon. The Book of Psalms consists of 150 hymns and prayers of which two examples are given below; the first describes an ethical basis that must be a fundamental pre-requisite for a wholesome and sustainable society, the second, Psalm 23 "The Lord is my Shepherd," is arguably the most famous of all of the psalms. For many people it has been a guiding light throughout their lives, and a constant source of comfort in difficult times:

PSALM 15

Lord, who may abide in your tabernacle?
Who may dwell in your holy hill?
He who walks uprightly, and works right-
    eousness,
And speaks the truth in his heart;
He who does not backbite with his tongue,
Nor does evil to his neighbor,
Nor does he take up a reproach with his
    friend;
In whose eyes a vile person is despised,
But he honors those who fear the Lord;

He who swears to his own hurt and does not
change;
He who does not put his money at usury,
Nor does he take a bribe against the
innocent.
He who does these things shall never be
moved.

PSALM 23

The Lord is my shepherd; I shall not want.
He makes me to lie down in green pastures;
He leads me beside the still waters. He
restores my soul;
He leads me in the paths of righteousness for
His name's sake.
Yea, though I walk through the valley of the
shadow of death,
I will fear no evil; for you are with me;
Your rod and your staff, they comfort me.
You prepare a table before me in the pres-
ence of my enemies;
You anoint my head with oil; my cup runs
over.
Surely goodness and mercy shall follow me
all the days of my life;
And I will dwell in the house of the Lord
forever.

It is clear that the golden thread of spiritual understanding, which from ancient times connected us to the spiritual world, wove its way down through ancient Egypt to Moses and the people of Israel, and then into Christianity. As Christianity emerged out of Judaism it was inevitable that early Christian religious life would continue to some degree the same practices and disciplines of Israel, consequently, many of the prayers used by early Christians were prayers used in common by both Jew and Christian. Thus, apart from the teachings of Jesus and His Apostles, the scriptures were then, as now, a major source of inspiration for many Christian prayers; however, the most important prayer in Christian terms has ever been, and always will be, the prayer taught by Jesus Christ himself.

Known as the "Pater Noster" or "The Lord's Prayer," it embodies the same essential relationship between humanity and the divine as established in Egyptian, Babylonian, Assyrian, and Jewish religions, of which it could be argued that Christianity is but a continuation. Yet, the Lord's Prayer contains an element that is unique in that it is accepted by all Christians as being given to humanity by God, rather than an entreaty from humanity to God. It is consequently far more intimate in its relationship than anything that man alone had previously devised, indeed, for countless people, both religious and secular, this prayer has been the focal point of prolonged contemplation; its simplicity should not be taken at face value. There also follows another early Christian prayer that is typical in that it demonstrates our perpetual need to involve the divine in our daily life.

THE LORD'S PRAYER

Our Father which art in heaven,
Hallowed be thy name.
Thy kingdom come, Thy will be done,
In earth as it is in heaven.
Give us this day our daily bread,
And forgive us our debts as we forgive our
    debtors,
And lead us not into temptation but deliver
    us from evil.
For thine is the kingdom and the power and
    the glory for ever.
Amen[13]

A Morning Prayer

Helper of Men who turn to you, Light of
    men in the dark,
Creator of all that grows that grows from
    seed,
Promoter of all spiritual growth, have mercy,
    Lord on me
And make me a temple fit for yourself.
Do not scan my transgressions too closely,
For if you are quick to notice my offences,
I shall not dare appear before you.
In your great mercy, in your boundless
    compassion,
Wash away my sins, through Jesus Christ,
Your only Child, the truly holy,
The chief of our souls' healers.
Through Him may all glory be given you,
All power and honour and praise,
Throughout the unending succession of ages.
Amen[14]

That same golden thread, which passed
through ancient Egypt and Israel and then into
Christianity, also flowed via Orpheus, Solon,
and Pythagoras into the world of classical
Greece, and thus to Rome. It is an obvious
thread, yet it has often been passed over unno-

ticed by those seeking evidence of deeper things, which does indeed exist, although not, as some might suppose, in the gloomy recesses of secret halls full of cryptic symbolism. Rather it is found in the relationship that exists between humanity and the divine; and is more commonly beheld in the highs and lows of daily life. For as creatures subject to the whims of fate, and suffering particularly from such constant threats to our very existence as disease, war, and famine, we commune more readily with the divine when under pressure or when threatened; as so much of human history testifies. The following hymn from ancient Greece is typical of that relationship, in that they are concerned with establishing and continuing a harmonious rapport between the gods and the community, that peace, prosperity, and health may be maintained.

HYMN OF THE KOURETES

Io, Kouros most great, I give thee hail,
    Kronian,
Lord of all that is wet and gleaming,
Thou art come at the head of thy
    Daimones.

That we make to thee with harps and pipes
    mingled together,
And sing as we come to a stand at thy well-
    fenced altar.
For here the shielded Nurturers took thee, a
    child immortal,
From Rhea, and with noise of beating feet
    hid thee away.
And the Horai began to be fruitful year
    by year
And Dike to possess mankind, and all wild
    living things
Were held about by wealth-loving Peace.
To us also leap for full jars, and leap for
    fleecy flocks,
And leap for fields of fruit, and for hives to
    bring increase.
Leap for our cities, and leap for our sea-
    borne ships,
And leap for our young citizens and for
    goodly Themis.[15]

And yet, as efficacious as such prayers might
be, it is nevertheless a matter of fact that just as
every life has its turn on the world stage, so
every civilization has its day and then declines
as another rises to take its place at the forefront

of the honors list, and so it was with classical Greece, which in its own fashion gave way to the emerging power of Rome. Initially the religion of Rome was a family religion, where each family constituted a little church whose center and focal point was Hestia (or Vesta), the goddess of the hearth. Upon this model the state religion of Rome was founded. Hestia was the guardian of family life both for the state and its citizens; a temple to Hestia stood in the center of Rome wherein burned a sacred fire that was never allowed to go out. However, if the Roman military conquered Greece, then Greek religion conquered Rome. Greece became the elderly tutor to the younger Rome, particularly where religion and philosophy were concerned. Greek anthropomorphism displaced Roman animism and their love of ritual, pomp, sacrament, and aestheticism overwhelmed the simpler Roman cult.

In time the prayers of Rome and Greece merged both in form and spirit, as the needs and pantheons of both were essentially the same. The following example is taken from one of four prayers found in Cato's[16] "Farm Almanack" and addressed to the god Mars, is typical of the Greco-Roman world. It illustrates the intrinsic sense of relationship that humanity had always shared with the divine and is wonderfully direct and purposeful.

Prayer at the Lustration of a Farm

O Father Mars, I pray and beseech of thee, that thou wouldst be well willing and propitious to me, to my house, to my dependents; and for this reason I have ordered that the suovetaurillia should be led around my fields, my land and my farm, that thou shouldst hold back, and drive away sickness, visible and invisible, desolation, ruin, damages and storm; and that thou shouldst cause to grow and prosper the fruits of the soil, the grain, the vineyards and the thickets; that thou shouldst keep in safety the shepherds and the sheep; that thou shouldst give prosperity and health to me, to my house and my dependents. For these reasons, and because, as I have said, I am lustrating and causing to be lustrated my farm, my lands and my fields, mayst thou be increased by this suovetaurillia which is being offered to thee. O Father Mars mayst thou be increased by this suovetaurillia which is being offered to thee.[17]

In this prayer, as with all of the foregoing, the relationship between humanity and the divine is clearly an important part of daily life. Perhaps this is because in the ancient world life was precarious, and people sought every advantage, alternatively, perhaps it is because there is something within each of us that intuits another realm of existence, and desires knowledge and experience of it, no matter how clumsy or naïve the means. How we describe that something may be open to discussion, but for all intents and purposes there is an innate need within us all to live our life in a spiritually meaningful context, which the rewards and distractions of this world do not fulfill. The desire to commune with the divine, then, is not so much a conceit or a delusion, as a primary instinct lying at the very roots of our being.

Thus, from a personal perspective prayer is far more meaningful than any dictionary or encyclopedia definition might suggest. It may be understood on one level as the natural expression of our need to commune with God, sharing our most intimate thoughts, hopes, aspirations, intentions, fears and doubts with our creator in the same way as children commune with parents, or lovers with one another.

And as we have seen, at a mundane level the prayers of humanity are concerned with very human needs. After all, we are gregarious creatures who generally seek fulfillment in communion with each other, so why not with God? Deprived of human company we sicken because communication is fundamental to a healthy and meaningful life, the lack of which can result in loneliness, depression, and other psychological disorders. The same may be said regarding a meaningful spiritual life. Deprived of the opportunity to communicate with the divine essence that we call God, who is the very source, ground, and destiny of our existence, we have no benchmark or polestar to set our life's course by and ill health may well occur in the form of self-obsession and the inevitable addiction to the basic human failings of avarice, gluttony, anger, and lust.

On the other hand, to know that we may commune unhindered with the essence of the created universe; to know that essence as God, who is ever attentive and sympathetic to our concerns; to know that we will always be heard in absolute confidentiality; to know that there is nothing that stands between us and that supreme godhead other than our own inhibitions, is to know that we are anchored securely and meaningfully in the cosmos. Thus, we can in this knowledge unfold our lives in a context that has purpose and meaning both within and beyond the constraints of the mundane world, and furthermore, live in harmony with every other creature that inhabits creation. But, such communication requires of us that we not only speak well but that we also listen well, and that we listen attentively with an inward ear, otherwise there is little possibility of the soul hearing the voice of the divine because the spiritual world does not announce its presence noisily, "as the babbling of baboons," but silently, like the falling of snow. Thus, if we would hear the voice of the spirit then we must disconnect, if but for a moment, from the internal chatter of the mind and listen attentively in the silence that ensues. In understanding this we may recognized, as did St. Paul, that a person contains two parts: the first part a terrestrial, mortal being and the second part a celestial, immortal being, the first a creature of earth and the second a creature of spirit, St. Paul alludes here to a great mystery concerning the means whereby the "man of dust" is transformed into the "heavenly man." It is a mystery that applies not only to our earthly life but also to our spiritual life, and prayer is essential to both, thus:

All flesh is not the same flesh, but there is one kind of flesh of men, another of animals, another of fish and another of birds. There are also celestial bodies and terrestrial bodies; but the glory of the celestial is one and the glory of the terrestrial is another. There is one glory of the sun, another glory of the moon, and another glory of the stars; for one star differs from another star in glory. So also is the resurrection of the dead. The body is sown in corruption, it is raised in incorruption. It is sown in dishonor, it is raised in glory. It is sown in weakness, it is raised in power. It is sown a natural body, it is raised a spiritual body. There is a natural body, and there is a spiritual body. And so it is written, "The first man Adam became a living being." The last Adam became a life-giving spirit. However the spiritual is not first, but the natural, and afterwards the spiritual. The first man was of the earth, made of dust; the second man is the Lord from heaven. As was the man of dust, so also are those who are made of dust; and as is the heavenly man, so also are those who are heavenly. And as we have borne the image of the man of dust, we shall also bear the image of the heavenly man (1 Corinthians 15:39-49).

Thus far we have only looked at prayer as it applies to our earthly life. However, when viewed in another light, those with eyes to see will know that prayer embodies both an art and a science. As an art it is the secret language of the soul—a language which synthesizes thought, image, and emotion in a manner that is best described as an alchemical process, enabling the soul to transcend the limitations of mundane existence. As a science it defines the formulae and techniques of transcending that mundane world, which is the world of the senses and all that such implies. Our perception of the mundane world is defined by the experiences we have via the senses, which shape both what we feel and what we think. It is the life of "the man of dust" alluded to by St. Paul.

This same insight is implied in the writings that were compiled by the followers of Orpheus, who understood that human nature consists of two distinct parts—a mortal physical nature, derived from the Titans, and an

immortal spiritual nature derived from Dionysus. Legend has it that the Titans, encouraged
by the goddess Hera, slew the infant god
Dionysus and consumed him, for which terrible deed Zeus slew them with his thunderbolt.
From their remains man was created: part
immortal and part mortal. From this premise
they taught that the body was the tomb or
prison of the soul, and that salvation was only
to be attained by overcoming the mundane
world, of which the body is a part. Consequently, the soul could only free itself by subli-
mating the passionate, titanic nature and
regenerating the divine Dionysian nature that
lies within, and prayer was an essential part of
that process. This is expressed clearly in the following Orphic hymn, which is obviously concerned with the life of the soul beyond the
mundane world and the influence of the physical body—St. Paul's "man of dust."

A CONFESSION

Lord of Europa's Tyrian line, Zeus-born,
    who holdest at thy feet
The hundred citadels of Crete, I seek to thee
    from that dim shrine,

Roofed by the Quick and Carven Beam, by
    Chalyb steel and wild bull's blood
In flawless joints of cypress wood made
    steadfast. There in one pure stream
My days have run, the servant I, Initiate of
    Idaen Jove;
Where midnight Zagreus roves, I rove; I have
    endured his thunder-cry;
Fulfilled his red and bleeding feasts; held the
    Great Mother's mountain flame;
I am set free and named by name a bacchus
    of the mailed priests.
Robed in pure white I have borne me clean
    from man's vile birth and coffined clay,
And exiled from my lips away touch of all
    meat where life hath been.[18]

A comparable understanding is to be found
in ancient Egypt. Indeed, the Pharaoh was
known as the Lord of the two lands, of Lower
and Upper Egypt, a title that has also been
described as a metaphor concerning the terrestrial and celestial world. Indeed, the larger part
of the religious life of Pharaonic Egypt was
concerned with the relationship between them,
and it is a matter of fact that no other civilization has demonstrated so much interest in the

comings and goings of the soul between them. In ancient Egypt it was understood that when a body died, a spiritual body could be raised up from it, through the power of prayer. This art was known only to the sacerdotal orders, whose rites and the teachings concerning this process, were maintained in the strictest secrecy. Few people were privy to their mysteries, although it is on record that several non-Egyptians were given access to them, Moses being one,[19] Orpheus another.[20]

The following is a prayer used in the making of a *Sahu* or spiritual body. It was believed that "If the prescribed prayers were said and the appropriate ceremonies were properly performed over the dead body by duly appointed priests, it acquired the power of developing from out of itself an immaterial body called a *Sahu* which was able to ascend to heaven and dwell with the gods therein."[21]

Homage to thee, O thou that dwellest in the holy mountain of Amentet. Osiris the royal Scribe Nekhtu-Amen, victorious, knoweth thee, and he knoweth thy name. Deliver thou him from the worms which are in Re-stau, which live upon the bodies of men and

women and which feed upon their blood, for
Osiris, the favoured one of the god of his
city, the royal scribe, Nekhtu-Amen, victorious, knoweth you, and he knoweth your
names. Let this be the first bidding of Osiris
Neb-er-tcher who keepeth hidden his body.
May he give air and escape from the Terrible
One who dwelleth in the Bight of the Stream
of Amentet, and may he decree the actions of
he that is rising up. Let him pass on to him
whose throne is within the darkness, who
giveth glory in Re-stau. O Lord of Light,
come thou and swallow up the worms which
are in Amentet. The great god who dwelleth
in Tattu, and who is unseen, heareth his
prayers, but those who are in affliction fear
him as he cometh forth with the sentence of
the divine block. I Osiris, the royal scribe
Nekhtu-Amen, have come bearing the decree
of Neb-er-tcher, and Horus hath taken pos-
session of his throne for him. His father, the
lord of those who are in the boat of father
Horus, hath ascribed praise unto him. He
cometh with tidings ... and may he see
Annu (Heliopolis). Their chief standeth upon
the earth before him, and the scribes mag-
nify him at the door of their assemblies, and

they bind his swathings in Annu. He hath led captive Heaven and he hath seized the earth in his grasp. Neither the heavens nor the earth can be taken away from him, for behold he is Ra, the first-born of the gods...[22]

Similarly, in ancient Greece, the Eleusinian Mysteries,[23] ancient before Pythagoras was born, were concerned with the philosophical death and subsequent regeneration of the soul as a spiritual or divine being. The sacred rites of Eleusius were so honored and respected throughout the ancient world that no one ever broke the code of silence imposed upon those initiated into these Mysteries thereof, although fortunately they were alluded to in a veiled way by several writers, including Aristophanes, Plato, and Plotinus. The following hymn concerns these mysteries. It is attributed to Orpheus, the acclaimed reformer of the Eleusinian Mysteries:

I shall utter to whom it is lawful;mbut let the door be closed, nevertheless, against all the profane. But do thou hear, Oh Musaeus, for I will declare what is true . . . He is the One, self-proceeding; and from him all things proceed, and in them he himself exerts his activity; no mortal beholds Him, but he beholds all. There is one royal body, in which all things are enwombed, Fire and Water, Earth, Aether, Night and Day, and Counsel [Metis], the first producer, and delightful Love—For all these are contained in the great body of Zeus. Zeus, the mighty thunderer, is first; Zeus is the last; Zeus is the head; Zeus is the middle of all things; from Zeus were all things produced. He is male, he is female; Zeus is the depth of the Earth, the height of the starry heavens; He is the breath of all things, the force of untamed fire; The bottom of the sea; Sun, Moon, and Stars; Origin of all; King of all; One Power, One God, One great Ruler.[24]

This hymn speaks plainly now of what was once a great mystery revealed only in metaphors and allegorical tales. Perhaps this was for the best. Perhaps, at first, it was the only way the integrity of the liturgy and the religious calendar could be sustained in a world where literacy was generally irrelevant. After all, the world had survived for millennia without the need for a literate society; relying instead on historians, priests, and poets who maintained reasonably accurate records in the form of stories and poems. However, times change, and with the introduction of an effective alphabet during the 6th or 7th century B.C. onward, more and more people learned the art of reading and writing.

The following instructions from the *Enneads* of Plotinus describe a means by which initiates could elevate their consciousness to experience something of the divine. In this instruction Plotinus alludes to a spiritual teaching that was probably central to the Mystery schools, not only of Eleusis, but of all the schools of that era:

On the Vision of God

Let us, then, make a mental picture of our universe: each member shall remain what it is, distinctly apart; yet all is to form, as far as possible, a complete unity so that whatever comes into view shall show as if it were the surface of the orb over all, bringing immediately the vision of the one plane, of the Sun and of all the stars with the earth and sea and all living things as if exhibited upon a transparent globe. Bring this vision actually before your sight, so that there shall be in your mind the gleaming representation of a sphere...

Keep this sphere before you, and from it imagine another, a sphere stripped of all magnitude and of spatial differences; cast out your inborn sense of Matter, taking care not merely to attenuate it: call on God, maker of the sphere whose image you now hold, and pray to Him to enter. And may He come bringing His own Universe with all the gods that dwelleth in it—He who is the One God and all the gods, where each is all, blending into a unity, distinct in powers but all one god in virtue of that one divine power of many facets. More truly this is the one God who is all the gods...[25]

The essence of Plotinus's teaching proposes three principal modes of being to which he applies the term "Hypostases." The first he defines as *The One,* which is the prime source and principle of all being, the very ground of existence. The second is the *Divine Nous* or Mind, in which exist the archetypal ideas and prototypes of all Creation. The third, proceeding from the Divine Nous, is the *World Soul*, below which lies the realm of Nature, which constitutes the outer life of the World Soul, and last of all there is undifferentiated Matter—the last consequence of the outpouring of the One; it forms the lowest stage of the universe, and is thus understood to be the antithesis of the One.

Plotinus taught that the World Soul consists of two parts. First, a higher celestial part through which it contemplates the Divine Nous; and second, a lower terrestrial part, through which it generates the material cosmos according to the archetypal model contained within the Divine Nous.

Human souls proceed from the World Soul, and like the World Soul may also be subdivided into two or more parts, for a human being, he taught, is a microcosm wherein the principles of the hypostases are reflected as spirit, soul, and body. Below the sphere of the soul lies the material world, in which the soul's conjunction with matter and a material body takes place, and which Plotinus taught was a fall or descent from a higher state of being. It is from this fall or descent that the soul seeks redemption, and, to which Plotinus devotes much of his attention.

Plotinus's model of the cosmos is significant, in that he describes in literal terms what previously had been taught through metaphor and allegory and only experienced by the initiate during the celebration of the Mysteries. At the center of this celebration, with all of its pomp, ceremonial, and drama, the consciousness of the initiate would have been elevated through the use of evocative prayer to experience the World Soul in the form of Demeter, and then after a different fashion, to experience the Divine Nous in the form of Dionysus. Plotinus believed that it was possible for individual souls, through the practice of contemplation, to rise to the level of the Divine Nous, and there, in spiritual union, be absorbed back into the One.

Plotinus describes what are effectively the most important objectives of the Mystery Schools, which were the direct experience of, and union with, divinity. The first part, often thought of as the "Lesser Mysteries," was concerned with the separation of the soul from the carnal nature of the physical body. The second part, often described in one way or another as

the "Greater Mysteries," was essentially concerned with the elevation of the soul beyond
the phrenic nature of the psychic world into the
presence of divinity. Similar processes may be
discovered in the mysteries of many cultures,
but particularly in the western line that flowed
out of ancient Egypt.

In some regions, the Western line, or tradition, interacted with other traditions. One such
interaction was with the cult of Mithras, a cult
that originally emerged out of the Persian religion of Zoroastrianism. In Rome the two
merged and the Mithraic Mysteries became a
fundamental part of Roman life. Little evidence
remains of the Mithraic cult and its mysteries,
other than the sculptures and inscriptions preserved in the ruins of its temples, and little of its
liturgy has survived. Yet, Mithraism was once
the religion of the Roman army with centers
throughout the Empire. Indeed, it can be
argued that if Constantine had failed in his
objectives, Mithraism, not Christianity, would
most probably have become the religion of the
Empire. However, Christianity triumphed and
in the centuries succeeding Constantine
Mithraism faded into obscurity, albeit with
some assistance from the Christian authorities.

The following prayer is taken from what is believed to be a rare surviving ritual from the Mithraic liturgy; it contains elements found in Egyptian, Judaic, and Greek prayers and hymns that suggest a comparable understanding of humankind's inherent spirituality.

MITHRAIC PRAYER OF INVOCATION

O Primal Origin of my origination; Thou Primal Substance of my substance; First Breath of breath, the breath that is in me; First Fire, God-given for the Blending of the blendings in me; First Fire of fire in me; First Water of my water, the water in me; Primal Earth-essence of the earthy essence in me; Thou Perfect Body of me—*name*—fashioned by Honoured Arm and Incorruptible Right Hand, in World that's lightless, yet radiant with Light, in World that's soulless, yet filled full of Soul! If verily, it may seem good to you, translate me, now held by my lower nature, unto the generation that is free from Death; in order that; beyond the insistent Need that presses on me, I may have vision of the Deathless Source, by virtue of the Deathless Spirit, by virtue of the Deathless

Water, by virtue of the Deathless Solid, and by virtue of the Deathless Air; in order that I may become reborn in Mind; in order that I may become initiate, and that the Holy Breath may breathe in me; in order that I may admire the Holy Fire; that I may see the Deep of the New Dawn, the Water that doth cause the Soul to thrill; and the Life-bestowing Aether which surrounds all things may give me hearing. For I am to behold today with Deathless eyes—I, mortal born of mortal womb, but now made better by the Might of Mighty Power, yea, by the Incorruptible Right Hand—I am to see today by virtue of the Deathless Spirit the Deathless Aeon, the Master of the Diadems of Fire—I with pure purities now purified, the human soul-power of me subsisting for a little while in purity; which power I shall again receive transmitted to me beyond the insistent Bitterness that presses on me, Necessity whose debts can never go unpaid—*name*—according to the Ordinance of God that naught can ever change. For that is beyond my reach that, born beneath the sway of Death, I should unaided soar into the Height, together with the golden sparklings of the Brilliancy that knows no Death. Stay still, O Nature doomed to perish, nature of men subject to Death! And straightway let me pass beyond the Need implacable that presses on me; for that I am His Son; I breathe; I am![26]

It is evident that from ancient times humanity recognized the spiritual dimension of life and sought to come into contact with it—an aspiration that inevitably evolved unique forms of expression according to the varying natures of different cultures. However, that was all to change as the ancient world was irrevocably transformed by the empire building of Alexander the Great, who gave the ancient world a new focal point and a common language that enabled the philosophical and religious beliefs of many cultures to interact. Alexander opened up the world in a way that was to have far-reaching effects, for within a century of his passing, Rome became the focal point of the known world and succeeded to much of Alexander's empire; subsequently, for more that five hundred years, "civilization" meant Roman civilization. During the first centuries of our era the Roman Empire had become a melting pot of countless speculative ideas and

belief systems, many of which were a potpour-
ri of spiritual ideals and dynamics compiled
from many sources and traditions. Out of this
melee Christianity emerged as the dominant
religious and political system. As times
changed the schools of the Mysteries disappeared, partly proscribed, and partly absorbed
into the mainstream of public religion; some
moving beyond the immediate reach of the
administration. The following hymn, written in
the late fourth century by St. Gregory
Nazianzen of Constantinople, clearly echoes
something of the Mystery Schools:

> O All-transcendent God (What other name
> describes you?)
> What words can sing your praises? No word
> at all denotes you.
> What mind can probe your secrets? No mind
> at all can grasp you.
> Alone beyond the power of speech, all men
> can speak of springs from you;
> Alone beyond the power of thought, all men
> can think of stems from you.
> All things proclaim You—things that can
> speak, things that cannot.

All things revere You—things that have reason, things that have none.
The whole world's longing and pain mingle
about you.
All things breathe you a silent prayer, a silent
hymn of your own composing.
All that exists you uphold, all things in con-
cert move to your orders.
You are the end of all that is, you are one,
you are all;
You are none of the things that are, you are
not a part and not the whole.
All names are at your disposal; How shall I
name you, the only unnameable?
What mind's affinities with heaven can
pierce the veils above the clouds?
Mercy, all-transcendent God, what other
name describes you?[27]

If there was a place where the ethos of the
mysteries survived, it was in the monasteries
that appeared with so much force and vitality
during the latter part of the fourth century.
These small communities of people, dedicated
to a life of prayer and meditation, contin-
ued the spiritual aspirations of the Mystery
Schools, but after a different fashion. Alas,

little of the schools has survived the test of time, except perhaps in the writings of Dionysius the Areopagite, otherwise known today as Pseudo-Dionysius, who is generally believed to have been a Syrian monk whose life spanned the end of the fifth and beginning of the sixth century. The Dionysian corpus consists of five titles: *The Divine Names; The Mystical Theology; The Celestial Hierarchy; The Ecclesiastical Hierarchy;* and *Epistles.* These profoundly influential books are not simply historical documents; they are essentially a spiritual teaching whose subject is the nature of the interior life of the soul and the permanent reality that is the substrate of its existence, and whose expression is an exquisite reflection of the mystical philosophy and spiritual life of the ancient world sublimated in Christianity. In the words of Dionysius himself;

> Unto this Darkness which is beyond Light we pray that we may come, and may attain unto vision through the loss of sight and knowledge, and that in ceasing thus to see or to know that which is beyond all perception and understanding (for this emptying of our faculties is true sight and knowledge), that

we may offer Him that transcends all things
the praises of a transcendent hymnody,
which we shall do by denying or removing
all things that are—like as men who, carving
a statue out of marble, remove all the imped-
iments that hinder the clear perspective of
the latent image and by this mere removal
display the hidden statue itself in its hidden
beauty.[28]

The influence of Plotinus, and indeed of
much of the ancient world, is obvious in the
Dionysian Corpus. Indeed, it may be said that
through this Syrian monk the ancient world
was able to pass on a most important legacy—
as many have since discovered. His work is a
call to a life of prayer and meditation beyond
the reaches of the mundane world, but this
does not exclude the majority of us of engaging
in prayer, nor of benefiting from what he has to
say. Remember, prayer is communing with God
and the only prerequisite is that we engage
attentively and with respect. However, prayer
does also lie at the heart of a sacred science of
spiritual development barely known beyond
the quiet waters of the sanctuary. This sacred
science requires spiritual tools and methods,

and in prayer we have the most useful and effective tool that we can ever hope for, because it is part of us and is both readily available and immediately accessible. Prayer is the means by which we can open the doorway of the sanctuary that lies within the hidden temple of the heart.

The obstacles that stand in the way of entering that inner temple and engaging in such prayer are the attitudes and preconceptions that form the major part of our self-image and worldview inherited from our family generic values and convictions concerning spiritual things, and our schooling and social connections contribute further. Inevitably, some of this conditioning, which at some point was useful to us, becomes redundant, yet we continue to hold onto it. Unfortunately, much of this redundant conditioning gleaned indiscriminately during formative years is little more than a medley of misconceptions and half-truths that have been maintained since childhood with such loyalty and determination that even in adulthood we frequently and often successfully, defend them against all reason. We forget, perhaps, that when we were children we were taught as children. The teachings we were given concerning the spiritual dimension of our existence, if indeed we were given any, were designed for the minds of children and not for the minds of adults. Thus our conception of God as we enter puberty is inevitably childish, and if at first we believe that God is perfect and omnipotent, we believe this as children and not as adults. As juveniles the incongruities in the world, particularly concerning injustice, suffering, warfare, and disease challenge our beliefs and turn many of us away from God. After all, if there is a God, then surely He would not allow injustice and suffering to exist, would He? For some of us these incongruities of the world are checked by a simple almost blind faith in what we have been taught, a naïve trust just waiting to be challenged. Thus armed with a juvenile view of the spiritual dimension of our existence, we sallied forth into adulthood.

However, the kind of prayer that opens the doorway of the inner temple requires something more than superstitious sentimentality and a vague belief in deity. It requires more than the mindless repetition of vaguely understood words, because prayer is first and foremost a personal relationship between the soul and God, therefore, the clearer the concept the soul has of "God," the more able is the soul to focus its attention upon God. Such an undertaking, when approached in the right way, is capable of releasing the soul from its prison of self-image. Consequently, one of the most important tasks we can undertake is the conscious development of a more mature concept of God. But, if we are to do this, then we must begin with acknowledging that God is not some vague abstraction or distant entity, but the source, ground, and destiny of our being, and that creation is both sane and full of love, proceeding in every detail as God planned it, and as such it is perfect. We may not understand that perfection, but then do we have a clear idea of what we mean by the term "perfect"? The word describes that which is complete and without flaw and as such in its absolute sense applies to God alone, for God is by definition that which is perfect. Unfortunately, all we can rely on to assist our judgment are relative correspondences and reference points gleaned from our life experiences, which are as yet insufficient for comprehending the absolute nature of God, and because of our incomplete understanding there is always the possibility of assuming that creation is like

God—in a state of absolute perfection, a condition that is obviously untrue.

Nevertheless, it is true to say that creation functions precisely as God intends, which is to say that the will of God is completely fulfilled in and by creation. Creation then is in perfect harmony with divine will and as such is completely without error, and is consequently without flaw, although it has yet to attain a state of ultimate or absolute Perfection. This idea is not so difficult to understand if we recognize that the Will of God is fulfilled in creation through the process we currently know as "evolution," a word that means "to unfold," although it is commonly used today by the exponents of Materialism as a term to describe the progressive development of creation from simple to more complex forms. Nevertheless, from a spiritual perspective, creation fulfills the Will of God by evolving to a predetermined goal as yet barely comprehended by humanity; for humanity, like the rest of creation, is evolving in accordance with God's Will, and has yet to attain the final state of absolute perfection that can give a complete understanding of the purpose and meaning of existence.

Prayer is also an art, an art that combines

thought and feeling in a manner that is best
summed up in the ancient formula "Inflame
thyself with prayer and invoke often." This
means that we should involve real feeling when
praying, for such prayer is a vehicle, which
under the right conditions, will bear the soul
aloft as if upon a magic carpet to higher and
more sublime levels of consciousness. Yet, for
so many people emotions are rarely experienced other than as a reaction to a specific
event, and more often than not are associated
with powerful and very physical sensations.
This is not surprising considering that society
barely recognizes the need for emotional development beyond the ability to function within
the normal constraints of everyday life. Such
primitive, self-focused conditioning limits the
potential for spiritual development in that it
imperceptibly supports egoism, which is the
antithesis of spiritual Gnosis. Selfless or
unselfish emotions, however, invariably involve
giving—the joy felt when a gift is well received
or when a deed is commended—and this ele-
vates the soul. The simple pleasure experienced
by everyday kindness inspires not only personal wellbeing but the desire for the wellbeing of
others, which is only a short step away from

fulfilling the Lord's wish that we do unto others as we would have them do unto us. Fulfilling this commandment is perhaps one of the most liberating steps we can take. It frees our thoughts and emotions from the selfish instinctive urges that dominate our life and engenders the realization that inasmuch as we are part of creation, we are a part of the Divine. It is in this ideal state that we can best direct our combined thoughts and feelings toward God. This chemistry of the very substance of the soul drives prayer, like Cupid's arrow, straight to its object of love—God.

In prayer the motive is of fundamental importance, for when prayer is directed toward spiritual development, its potential for effect is maximized, but when directed towards material objectives its potential is minimized. This must be understood in the context of the purpose of our existence, which we are taught is to seek the kingdom of heaven (Matt. 6:33). Seeking the "kingdom" is essentially an inner or supernatural quest that takes the seeker beyond the world of the senses into realms where there are more important factors to be considered than the demands of our worldly needs. In this interior world, the soul discovers how its earthly experience is merely a reflection of events taking place therein. Such wisdom that may be gained in this world is gained through prayer because in this spiritual environment prayer has a direct and immediate influence as it is essentially of the same spirit and nature of the substance found therein. However, expecting changes to be made in the exterior world of the senses through our prayers would be imprudent, as that would require altering the patterns established by natural law, which is most unlikely to succeed *directly*. That it is noble to pray for the material wellbeing of others—praying for their health and safety, praying that they may have sufficient for their needs, or that they may live in peace without threat or hindrance—is highly commendable and not to be underestimated, for although our prayers may not have any obvious or direct effect, they still have the power to influence, *indirectly*.

To understand this point, consider as an example a typical situation where our prayers may be called upon: a country is in political turmoil, its government is using extremely harsh measures in attempting to establish some kind of order. The consequence of this is that many people are being imprisoned, tortured, or killed indiscriminately by some or all of the factions involved. The economy is in a state of collapse, food production has ceased, and famine and disease threaten. This is a very real situation in many countries today and is a situation that demands from any sensitive individual that the very least they could do, apart from giving material assistance, is to *pray* for peace and order to be restored. It may not seem very much, but the consequence of the combined prayers of many individuals intent upon the same objective generates a force that will influence the hearts and minds of those involved in such conflicts with a real desire for peace. This *indirect* but powerful influence is generated by prayer offered to God on their behalf, because when our prayers are offered to God, they are transformed from a *partisan* goodwill into a *universal* expression of divine love. In this elevated and transformed state, the essence of our prayer becomes acceptable to the souls involved in such conflicts. Through the power and love of the divine and in accordance with natural law, the moderating influence of our prayers is able to assist reason and compassion to overcome hatred and the desire for revenge.

Thus, in due course, peace and order are restored. The scale is irrelevant, whether it is one person praying for another, or a small group praying for world peace: no effort is futile.

When prayer is directed toward spiritual development its effectiveness is unquestionable. For when the soul is truly caught up in prayer it is in communion with the divine, which communicates with the soul by transforming thought into realization. Doubt blows away like chaff before the wind, thought ceases and consciousness leaps the barriers separating it from its source. The soul is nourished by the radiant light of pure love and in this blessed light grows strong in holiness. Then the delusion of separateness fades away allowing Truth to filter through the coarse fibers of its earthbound consciousness and stimulate the seed of Gnosis. Prayer of this nature requires commitment to its development. Its immeasurable potential is realized only through regular practice. There are no shortcuts or easy options when dealing with such prayer for it is the secret language of the soul, and consists not merely of words but of a chemistry of being, a chemistry that combines concentration, purity of intention, emotional control, clarity of thought, and humility.

The time and place are also of great importance—a quiet place free from interruption where you may gather your thoughts and *be still* as the Lord taught. Turning within and fixing your attention upon the light within the inner temple, it is possible to perceive a great truth underlying the dynamics of this chemistry; a truth that not only reveals the essential commonality of the human spirit, but also reveals the true nature of the Self. Unfortunately many prefer to avert their gaze when thus confronted, for old tribalisms linger in the memory and take a long time to change, especially when the will to change is reluctant. This is a great shame because the answer to many of our problems lies in discovering this inner reality. Thus, when Dudley Wright wrote, "Prayer is not the condescension of the Eternal to the human, but rather the ascension of the human towards union with the Eternal,"[29] he revealed a fundamental truth that so many have either forgotten or have never realized. Indeed, our civilization has for so long thought of prayer as being simply a petition from the weak to the strong, from the poor to the wealthy, from the meek to the powerful, that the essence and purpose of prayer has long been hidden behind a veil of misconceptions. Consequently, in this increasingly secular world, the use of prayer declines while the need for meaning in life grows ever more urgent.

With this book, Dudley Wright re-opens a door that gives us access to a greater world of consciousness than we commonly imagine and enables people to articulate their spiritual life in a meaningful and wholesome context. It is a door through which the emancipation of the soul is attained not through denying or rejecting the divine, but in engaging and communing with it. Dudley Wright reminds us that the mundane world is not the only world for we are not only children of earth but also "of Starry Heaven." Indeed, "Our race is of Heaven alone," for the divine is the source, ground, and destiny of our being, and it is in that alone we shall find the context and meaning of our life.

The mind is a garden named delight,
Wherein God dwells concealed from sight.
Therein pray, as did Jesus before Easter day.
Then thou shalt know, with vision clear,

That Heaven's within us now and here.
Sorrows on earth shall sometime cease,
In the presence of the Lord of Peace;
For He has risen, that we may be
One with Him Eternally.[30]

Allan Armstrong,
Prior of the Order of Dionysis & Paul
Bristol, England, July 2004

NOTES

1. The basic premise of Materialism is that physical matter is all that there is—it is the only reality. Consequently, all aspects of the universe, including life in its many forms, are explainable in material terms.

2. Desiderius Erasmus (1466–1536) was one of the most important literary figures of the Renaissance period. His best known work is the *Praise of Folly*, a pamphlet directed against the vanities of the ruling classes and church. He devoted himself to the revision of Christian traditions, fighting for a clearer and more humane approach of religion.

3. Sir Thomas More (1478–1535), later canonized St. Thomas More, is famous for his book *Utopia* (1515) and for his martyrdom. As Chancellor to Henry VIII, he refused to sanction Henry's divorce of Queen Catherine. More was imprisoned, tried, and executed. More was a friend of such Renaissance humanists as Erasmus, John Colet, and Thomas Linacre.

4. Marsilio Ficino (1433–1499), the Florentine, was a man who wrought a deep and lasting change in European society. From him and his Academy, the Renaissance drew its most potent intellectual and spiritual inspiration. To Ficino, the writings of Plato and his followers contained the key to the most important knowledge for humankind: that is, knowledge of the divine and immortal principle within the human.

5. Leucippus was the originator of the Atomic Theory; he lived in the second half of the fifth century B.C.

6. Democritus of Abdera (460–357 B.C.) was a student of Leucippus and proponent of the Atomic Theory.

7. Thomas Hobbes' (1588–1679) philosophy is perhaps the most complete materialist philosophy of the 17th

century. He rejected Cartesian dualism and believed in the mortality of the soul. He rejected free will in favor of a determinism which treats freedom as being able to do what one desires. He rejected Aristotelian and scholastic philosophy in favor of the philosophy of Galileo and Gassendi, which largely treats the world as matter in motion.

8. Sir E. A. Wallis Budge, trans., *The Book of the Dead* (London, 1899), p. 327.

9. Budge, *The Book of the Dead*, p. 63.

10. Stephen Langdon, *The Mythology of All Races: Semitic Mythology* (Boston: Rowman and Littlefield, 1931), p. 125.

11. S. H. Hooke, *Babylonian & Assyrian Religion* (Oxford: Basil Blackwell, 1962), pp. 101–102.

12. 1 Kings 8:23–29.

13. Matt. 6:9–13

14. Adalbert Hamman, ed., *Early Christian Prayers* (Chicago: Franciscan Herald Press, 1961) pp. 62–63.

15. Jane Harrison, *Themis* (London: Merlin Press, 1963), pp. 8–9.

16. Marcus Pocrius Cato, 234–149 B.C., was a Roman tribune.

17. Quoted in James Hastings, *Encyclopaedia of Religion & Ethics*, Vol. X (Edinburgh: T & T Clark, 1918), p. 200.

18. Jane Harrison, *Prolegomena* (London: Meridian Books, 1963) p. 479.

19. St. Paul informs us that Moses was learned in all the wisdom of Egypt (Acts 7:22); see also C. D. Yonge, *The Works of Philo* (Peabody, MA: Hendrickson, 1993), pp. 461–462

20. C. H. Oldfather, *Diodorus of Sicily,* vol. 1, (London: William Heinemann, 1933).

21. Budge, *The Book of the Dead,* p. lviii.

22. Ibid., p. 47.

23. Eleusinian Mysteries were based at Eleusius, the most important town in Attica after Athens and Piraeus. Renowned throughout antiquity, the mysteries were celebrated in honor of Demeter, Persephone, and Dionysus.

24. Thomas Taylor, *The Eleusinian & Bacchic Mysteries* (New York: J. W. Bouton, 1875), p. 166.

25. Stephen MacKenna and B. S. Page, trans., *Plotinus: The Six Enneads* (Chicago: Encyclopedia Britannica, 1952), Fifth Ennead, tractate VIII, Ch. 9, p. 245.

26. G.R.S. Mead, *Echoes From the Gnosis,* vol. VI: *A Mithraic Ritual* (London: Theosophical Society, 1907), pp. 18–21.

27. Hamman, *Early Christian Prayers*, p. 162.

28. Ibid., p. 194.

29. Dudley Wright, *Prayer* (Berwick, ME: Ibis Press, 2004), p. 107.

30. A verse by Mar Francis of the Holy Celtic Church.

THE UNIVERSALITY
OF PRAYER

T IS REFRESHING TO FIND IN THAT fascinating study of Comparative Religions one point, at least, upon which the adherents of nearly all forms of belief throughout the ages have found agreement— the necessity and efficacy of prayer, in spite of the many variations encountered in form and practice. So far as it is possible to trace, there never was a time when man did not, consciously or unconsciously, pray, and the objections which have been levelled against the act have, in general, resulted from the false applications of prayer by well-meaning, but unthinking and illogical, devotees.

The universality of the act of prayer is not difficult to prove. Forms of prayer have been discovered in Egyptian papyri, on Babylonian tablets, and in the rituals of ancient sorcerers. The *Iliad* of Homer and the *De Corona* of

Demosthenes began with invocations for heavenly assistance.

The objections to prayer are not of recent origin, and nearly one hundred and fifty years since the Rev. Richard Price, D.D., F.R.S., published a dissertation on prayer, in which he said: "There is no religious duty against which more objections have been raised." With the exception mentioned, the utility of prayer has scarcely been called into question, and the sceptic has frequently been compelled to acknowledge the potency of this spiritual act and its power over the life and conduct of the individual. It is stated that Voltaire left the house of Fenelon, where he was on a visit, lest he should become converted to the beliefs of his host because of his prayerful life; also that Voltaire himself, on one occasion, when in sudden danger, cast aside his theories, gave way to the natural tendency of the inner nature of man, and prayed—a proof that the Bishop of London was not far wrong when he declared that "man is a praying animal."

Dr. Farnell, in his work on *The Evolution of Religion*, has said that "There is no part of the religious service of mankind which reflects so vividly the material and psychological history of man as the formula of prayer."

There is, however, the false as well as the true application of prayer. The Thugs, before setting out on their garrotting expeditions, would pray, even as to-day the gangs of banditti will pray for success to attend them as they seek to waylay and rob the traveller. Fudhayl ben Ayaz, afterwards one of the Moslem saints, was, in his earlier days, a highwayman, and he collected around him a gang of robbers, of which he became the chief. It is recorded that he never neglected saying the Friday prayers, and dismissed any of his servants whom he found neglecting this religious exercise. His calling, and his practice in connection therewith, were entirely in opposition to the faith and practice of Islam; for, although the Moslem religion lays great stress upon the observance of ritual in prayer, it also emphasises the fact that the life and spirit of prayer is the inward disposition of the heart, and that the most punctilious observance of external rites and ceremonies is of little or no avail if performed without due attention to reverence, devotion, and hope. The fifth Sura (or chapter) of the

Koran also enjoins that the hands of a thief, whether man or woman, are to be cut off when the article stolen is of a greater value than forty shillings—a punishment which is not now inflicted. Prayer among all nations and peoples, tribes and sects, particularly the Roman Catholic, has often been a synonym for bribery offered to the Supreme, and men have promised to perform certain deeds and bestow benefactions, conditionally upon answers to their prayers being granted.

Socrates was, perhaps, the first philosopher to emphasise the spiritual view of prayer, and one of his petitions was, "Grant me to become noble of heart." The burden of Socrates' prayers was always that he might lead a virtuous and tranquil life; and both he and Plato understood prayer to be a communing with the gods, in order that they might practise virtue. This was the true Vedantist idea, and one of the prayers in the *Rig Veda* (viii. 19-2) runs: "O Lord, purify us with water, purify us with solar rays, purify us with medicinal herbs, and above all, purify us with Wisdom, endow us with Powers of Mind by enlightening our intellects."

Socrates' high altitude was maintained in pre-Christian ages, and preserved by some, at least, of the early Christian philosophers. According to Origen, the final justification for prayer was communion with God; and Clemens maintained that the true Gnostic, he who has the true knowledge of God, "works himself with God in his prayer, so as to attain perfection."

One false view of prayer is that the act must necessarily be confined to petition, and, generally, for asking for all kinds of material things of which we believe we stand in need, which, like the prayer for alterations or deviations of physical law, has excited the derision of the sceptic. Even some followers of the Vedas thought prayer could be employed to obtain terrestrial benefits: rain, sunshine, heat, etc.; and petitional prayer in this sense was the characteristic of many of the ancient forms of religion. The Manichean religion enjoined frequent fasts and four prayers daily to the sun and moon, which, however, were not worshipped as gods, but revered as manifestations of light. Some of these prayers, which have been preserved, have been found to be closely akin to certain Babylonian hymns.

The Shintoist regards it as sufficient merely to frame the wish, without giving it utterance, and, on rising in the morning, will turn towards the sun, rub the hands together, and bow.

Prayer is at once a point of resemblance and difference in the Christian and Islamic faiths. The followers of both claim to be praying people. Indeed, the Moslems have altered one of the verses of a well-known Christian hymn and caused it to read:

"Prayer is the Moslem's vital breath, The Moslem's native air,

His watchword at the gates of death; He enters heaven with prayer."

Prayer is enjoined upon the faithful Moslem five times daily between dawn and nightfall, and one cannot but admire his complete dissociation from his surroundings, whether the prayers be uttered in the Mosque, the open street, on board a vessel, or in the cemetery, and his entire disregard of the observations of other people, a characteristic which led to the following lines being written:

Most honour to the men of prayer,
Whose Mosque is in them everywhere!
Who, amid revel's wildest din,

In war's severest discipline,
On rolling deck, in thronged bazaar,
In stranger land, however far,
However different in their reach
Of thought, in manners, dress, or speech—
Will quietly their carpet spread,
To Mecca turn the humble head,
And, as if blind to all around,
And deaf to each distracting sound,
In simple language God adore,
In spirit to His presence soar,
And in the pauses of the prayer,
Rest as if wrapt in glory there.

Far, however, from regarding prayer as a vehicle or means for causing any deviation of natural law, the great characteristic of the faith of Islam is resignation to the will of God. Draper has pointed out in his *Conflict between Religion and Science* that "The prayer of the Christian was merely an intercession for benefits hoped for, that of the Saracen a devout expression of gratitude for the past." But neither Christian nor Moslem, however, seems to have grasped the true meaning of prayer.

Some people, while acknowledging the potency of prayer, yet look upon it as to be regarded merely as a secondary force; and we not infrequently hear the expression, "If you cannot do anything else, you can pray," whereas we ought never to forget that "whatever else we may do we must pray." It may not always be possible to demonstrate the efficacy of prayer to another, for the simple reason that there are some things which can never be proven, they can only be known; but, apart from all tangible evidence, no one who has been in the habit of enjoying intimate communion with the Unseen by means of prayer, will ever forget the effect such communion had upon his life and conduct.

ROMAN CATHOLICISM
AND PRAYER

ANY OF THE MOST EARNEST PRAYING souls the world has ever known have been members of that Church to which Macaulay paid more than one tribute of admiration, and several of the classical treatises on prayer have been written by the holy men and women who found refuge there and who could have found it nowhere else.

Miss H. H. Colvill, the biographer of Saint Teresa, relates that the saint learned from a book which she had read—Osuna's *Tercer Abecedario*—that the most effectual way to enter into the contemplative life was by prayer, not the petitional prayer, but prayer in its widest sense: "Mental Prayer, the Prayer of Recollection, a 'gathering up' of the spirit into a single purpose, a single consciousness, a pure, unmixed, undistracted contemplation of the divine, a deliberate and definite attempt to enter into direct communion with God."

Later on, Miss Colvill tells us that Saint Teresa "analyses minutely and distinguishes between the different stages of prayer. Beginning with deliberate and systematic meditation, it passes involuntarily and by degrees into the condition of Ecstasy and Rapture; the earliest stage of which, called the Prayer of Quiet, is accompanied by great peace and joy, and is not very uncommon among the religious of all sects who expect and welcome it. But Teresa passed beyond this Prayer of Quiet, through definite stages to the deeper and stranger rapture called the Prayer of Union."

Meditation, however, is not the initial stage. It can only be practised by those who have made some advance in the spiritual or higher life, and other writers of the Catholic Church have also set forth the various steps leading up to, and even beyond, it.

Father Benedict Canfield, a Capuchin Friar and Mystic, classified prayer under four headings or categories:

First.—Vocal Prayer, which he described as the most imperfect kind, because it has the

smallest measure of light, but is suitable for novices and beginners.

Second. —Mental Prayer, which is more advanced than the former, as denoting the presence of more light.

Third.—Aspirational Prayer, made with less labour of the understanding and characteristic of much progress.

Fourth.—A settled cleaving to the will of God alone, without meditation or vocal prayer.

This last should be the ultimate aim and object of all prayer, to bring ourselves *en rapport*, as it were, with the will of the Supreme Power. "Ask what ye will, and it shall be done unto you," is a promise sometimes claimed when the immediately preceding words, "If ye abide in me and my words abide in you," are overlooked or forgotten.

The four degrees of prayer of Father Canfield, already mentioned, are analogous with those of Saint Teresa, which she compared with four methods of watering a garden, each easier than the preceding. "The first, by drawing water from a well, which is severe labour; the second, by drawing it up by means of a hydraulic machine, in which way there is obtained, with less fatigue, a greater quantity of water; the third, by conducting the water from a river or brook; the fourth, and incomparably the best, is an abundance of rain, God Himself under-taking the watering without the slightest fatigue on our part."

Abbot Cisernoa, a Benedictine, also drew up a book of *Spiritual Exercises* divided into the threefold way of Purification, Illumination, and Union, a plan also followed by the Carthusian

Prior Michael of Coutances, forty-fifth General of the Carthusian Order.

Cardinal Bellarmine's *Eight Virtues of Conditions of True Prayer* were the following:

1. Faith (Matthew xxi. 22; Mark xi. 23);
2. Hope and Confidence (James i. 5–7);
3. State of Grace or Love of God;
4. Humility;
5. Devotion (1 Corinthians xiv. 15);
6. Perseverance;
7. Made for oneself;
8. Made for what is necessary or useful for salvation.

Dr. F. W. Faber, the Oratorian, distinguished between the Sulpician and Ignatian methods of prayer. The Sulpician method is a more faithful transcript of the tradition of the old Fathers and the saints of the desert, but both methods have meditation for their aim and object, which is regarded as a gift for which special prayer must be made.

The *Spiritual Exercises of St. Ignatius* form a perfect and complete compendium of prayer and meditation, and is one of the principal textbooks used in the education of every Jesuit priest in all parts of the world, as well as of other regular and secular priests, and not a few of the laity of the Roman Catholic Church.

Coming to more modern times, the lamented Father George Tyrrell will be remembered for at least many years to come by his philosophical-religious work *Lex Orandi*, wherein he says:

"Obviously, then, it is by conduct, but, primarily, by prayer in its widest sense, that this union with the Divine Will is fostered and the soul established and strengthened by, the sense of its solidarity with the entire Will-world as systematised through Him Who is its in-dwelling source and end. Union with any part of it that is separated from Him must, in the end, lead to an absolute solitude of the soul, unloved and unloving, shut apart into that outer darkness, which is spiritual death.

"Prayer, as here taken, is not merely directed to conduct, but is itself directly effective of that will-sympathy with God which is the richest fruit, as it is also the highest motive, of conduct. The religious effort is directed explicitly to the adjustment of our will to God's."

Vocal prayer may be regarded as a help

towards concentration and meditation, but the disciple must be careful not to loiter in the path, or, as Madame Guyon expressed it, "not become attached to the accommodation on the road, external practices, which must all be left behind when the signal is given."

Many of the forms of devotion in general use among Catholics, however, particularly the hurried manner in which the words are uttered, so that they become absolutely unintelligible to an ordinary and uninitiated spectator, seem to be of little profit, although it must be admitted that the same devotional spirit that characterises the Moslem is as strongly displayed by the Catholic, and that without any laboured effort. The beautiful liturgy of the Mass, the Angelus, and other devotions are invariably hurried through at the same break-neck speed, which is only beaten by the rate at which many clerics skim over the face of the words of their "office."

PRAYERS FOR THE DEAD AND
PRAYERS TO SAINTS

HALL WE ONLY PRAY FOR THOSE WHO are dwellers on this material plane of consciousness, or are we also to include in our petitions those who have passed away from our presence to other realms? Jews, Catholics, Ritualists, Mohammedans, Spiritualists, and others believe in and follow the practice of praying for those who have crossed the Borderland. If we believe in the persistence of life and personality, knowledge and progression of character, we shall unhesitatingly answer in the affirmative.

The contention of Spiritualism is that the so-called dead can be helped by prayer even more effectually than the living, by reason of the fact that we are able to reach their spiritual nature without encountering any physical barrier or obstruction. "Of the dead speak (or think) no ill," because a thought to those who have left the physical world is as quickly perceived by them as words are by those on earth. Our departed friends may also help us, as F. W. H. Myers points out in *Human Personality* (vol. ii. page 314): "We already have friends who help us on earth; those friends survive bodily death, and are, to some extent, able to help us still. It is for us to throw ourselves into the needed mental state, to make the heartfelt and truthful appeal."

Osiris, when in mortal form, is said to have frequently prayed to the gods for aid and for blessings to rest upon those who, ferried by Charon, had crossed the river Styx. The Cretans prayed to Jupiter and other gods to aid the living and the dead. Xenophon testifies that Cyrus prayed for the heroes that had fallen on his battlefield. St. Hilary, who wrote about 315 A.D., says: "There are many spiritual powers that are called angels and the spirits of the just who preside over churches and persons. They pray for us and we pray for the dead."

Life, and its powers, in the opinion of a daily increasing number of people, does not cease at the change of death. It is natural for us to ask for help or a favour from our living friends, and often, in mundane matters, we are more or less

dependent upon some one in particular, and it is natural to think and believe that if life thus continues, they retain their interest in us, even though we may miss their bodily presence. "We are in the midst of an invisible world of energetic and glorious life, a world of spiritual beings than whom we have been for a little while lower. That region or condition of space in which the departed find themselves immediately after death is probably much nearer than we imagine, for St. Paul speaks of us as being surrounded by a cloud of witnesses."

Father Sidney Smith, a Jesuit priest, has also given four reasons why prayer should be offered to saints direct, three of which are as follows:

1. The saints in heaven make assiduous intercession for us their brethren still struggling below on earth;

2. They are not without a particular knowledge of our wants and necessities;

3. We may, therefore, lawfully and profitably invoke them.

Jacob is said to have prevailed in prayer because he had power with the gods (*Elohim*— Genesis xxxii. 28).

It is unseemly to give way to excessive grief when our loved ones are called away, although we may greatly miss them. We may retard their progress in the Beyond by our grief, or we may help them by our prayers and loving thoughts, and may show our sincere repentance for any injury we may have done them by sending out our thoughts to wish them God-speed and progress in the higher realms.

Just as we by our prayers may influence for
good others who are on this material plane of
consciousness, so we may also be the subjects
of influence from the inhabitants of other
spheres. We read in Luke xxii. that when the
disciples followed Jesus to the Mount of Olives
and He had bidden them pray that they might
not enter into temptation, He Himself kneeled
down in the act of prayer, when there appeared
a messenger from the higher spheres strengthening Him. Everyone who would rise to the
stature of perfect manhood must attain, as a
step in the process, to the crucifixion of the carnal self, and, in this and all upward efforts, we
are aided, just as Jesus is said to have been, by
those angels or messengers of light, those com-
municating intelligences who help us to bridge
the gulf between the seen and the unseen.

Dr. Alfred Russel Wallace, in his work on
Miracles and Modern Spiritualism, maintains
that "The recently discussed question of the
efficacy of prayer receives a perfect solution by
Spiritualism. Prayer may be often answered,
though not directly by the Deity. Nor does the
answer depend wholly on the morality or religion of the petitioner; but as men who are both
moral and religious, and are firm believers in a

Divine response to prayer, will pray more frequently, more earnestly, and more disinterestedly, they will attract towards them a number of spiritual beings who sympathise with them, and who, when the necessary mediumistic power is present, will be able, as they are often willing, to answer the prayer."

Sir Oliver Lodge has said: "If we are open to influence from earth, other than by non-corporeal methods, may we not be open to influence from beings in another region or of another order? And, if so, may we not be aided, inspired, and guided? It is not a speculation only, it is a question for experiment to decide."

There are many who have decided the question from experience, and are able to assert confidently that they are assisted and directed in their prayerful aspirations by the inhabitants of the celestial spheres. Persistent seclusion from the world for the purpose of prayer is not necessary, although occasional or periodical retirement is, at least, helpful. One can, however, be in solitude in the busy street or the crowded hall—alone, yet not alone, because always accompanied by, and sometimes conscious of, the presence of our spirit comrades, the messengers of the Eternal.

PRAYER AND THERAPEUTICS

AS PRAYER ANY VALUE IN THERAPEU-
TICS? Can we, through the agency of
prayer, effect any alleviation of disease? At one of the annual meetings of the
British Medical Association, Dr. Theodore B.
Hyslop, superintendent of the Bethlem Royal
Hospital for the Insane, bore testimony to the
therapeutical value of prayer in the following
words: "As one whose whole life has been concerned with the sufferings of the mind, I would
state that of all hygienic measures to counteract
disturbed sleep, distressed spirits, and all the
miserable sequels of a distressed mind, I would
undoubtedly give the first place to the simple
habit of prayer."

M. Marcel Mangin contributed an article to
the *Annals of Psychical Science* for February
1908, upon *The Lourdes Cures and Metapsychical Science*, in which he gave full details of
several well-observed cases, and expressed his

inability to understand why miraculous cures had not been more studied, since miraculous healing is one of the most astounding facts of metapsychicism. The subject has, of course, been studied to a certain degree, and Mr. F. W. H. Myers, in conjunction with his brother, Dr. A. T. Myers, in 1893, published a work on *Mind Cure, Faith Cure and the Miracles of Lourdes*. In discussing the causes of the cures, M. Mangin concluded: "And prayer, I shall be told, you do not mention it? But I believe implicitly in the power of prayer. At Lourdes, the act of faith, whether it comes from the patient or a person interested in him, is the point of departure of all the influences I have been speaking about. The efficaciousness of prayer is one of the most admirable chapters in the history of mental suggestion, at no matter what distance."

Are such cures to be limited to those professing the Christian faith? Dr. Buckley, in an article in the *Century Magazine* for June 1885, contended that cures could be effected in Buddhist temples, Mohammedan mosques, Catholic and Protestant churches, and, indeed, anywhere indiscriminately, wherever people exercised faith, even in an unknown or utterly mistaken conception of Deity; and in the June–July 1908 issue of the *Annals of Psychical Science*, Mr. Byramji Hormusji wrote an article on "Andambar, the Indian Lourdes." Andambar is a village in the southern Mahratta country, and the scenes he describes can be witnessed there every week. There are four such resorts in Northern India, dedicated to the Hindu God, Dat-rat-rija, in whose name the various cures are effected. At this weekly festival, held every Thursday evening from eight to eleven o'clock, it is the custom to carry the palanquin of the god around the temple precincts. People come from all parts of the Deccan, bringing relatives or friends afflicted with one or other of the strange maladies not understood by medical science—epilepsy, hysteria, obsession, periodical madness, etc., and Mr. Hormusji gave details of cures from these diseases, and leprosy in addition.

Although many may claim to follow the teachings of the New Testament, there are some who would exclude from spiritual benefits those who do not see eye to eye with them. Such should remember the words of the Master: "Not every one that saith unto me, 'Lord, Lord,' shall enter into the kingdom of heaven, but he that doeth the will of my Father, who is in heaven"; and "Whoever shall do the will of my Father, the same is my brother, and sister, and mother," lest they receive the same rebuke that the apostles received as recorded in Mark ix. 38.

Luther prayed for Melancthon and he recovered, and many before and since that incident have prayed for restoration to health and strength of themselves and others with equally satisfactory results. Disease is not in accordance with natural law, but a disturbance of it. May it not be, as Thomas Lake Harris has said, that "Diseases in the body are correspondences of evil in the will," and that "Prayer is fruitful," *vide* Bishop Gore, "and is offered in spirit and truth, exactly as it is an attempt to correspond or cooperate with the purpose of God." By the exercise of this power we may bring others on to a higher plane and so raise them above their weakness and degradation.

The joint authors of *Religion and Medicine* state that "Prayer has a regenerating and uplifting effect on character; but, in affecting character it must also affect the nervous system. It does not seem irrational to believe that prayer opens the inner consciousness to the absorption of spiritual energy, by which, as philosophy assures us, the universe is sustained. And this attitude of receptivity towards the highest things in turn affects character and life, and the calm and purified spirit acts on the nervous organisation, restoring its tone and rhythm."

There is a certain force or power which affects everyone on entering a Catholic Church, even the individual who would repudiate the suggestion of being religious. Whence comes this power? I believe it arises mainly from the intense earnestness of the prayers offered up therein and the concentration of thought exerted. The same effect is not produced on entering a Nonconformist place of worship or a Jewish synagogue, and the defect here may also, I think, be accounted for by the lack of such earnestness and concentration. Conversation before and after the services upon worldly or trivial matters is by no means unknown to the worshippers in Nonconformist buildings, while in Jewish synagogues, even on solemn festivals, I have listened to audible conversation upon topics of business, horse racing, family and other matters, entirely dissociated from the purpose for which the synagogue was opened. It is scarcely necessary to say that such practice is entirely opposed to the spirit of Judaism, but it must have been rife even in the days of Moses Maimonides, for the great Jewish commentator drew attention to it in the following words:

"If we pray with the motion of our lips, and our face towards the wall, but, at the same time, think of our business; if we read the Law with our tongue, whilst our heart is occupied with the building of our house, and we do not think of what we are reading; if we perform the commandments only with our limbs, we are like those who are engaged in digging in the ground, or hewing wood in the forest, without reflecting on the nature of those acts, or by whom they are commanded, or what is their object. We must not imagine that in this way we attain the highest perfection; on the contrary, we are then like those in reference to whom Scripture says, 'Thou art near in their mouth, and far from their reins.'"

With regard to the Roman Catholic faith there can be no doubt that the intense belief in the doctrine of Transubstantiation is a powerful incentive to such earnestness and concentration of which I speak.

What is the cause of the occasional revival of so-called evangelical religion and of the spread of Roman Catholicism in Protestant countries? Not so much the direct result of intellectual conviction, as of concentration of thought and prayer, both individual and federated. The advent of the late D. L. Moody to London was traced to the persistent prayer of an elderly invalid lady in a northern suburb of the metropolis. In the Roman Church there are several large associations and confraternities in various parts of the world, particularly in the United Kingdom, existing for the sole object of praying for the conversion of Britain to the ancient faith, and special services are held monthly with this aim in nearly every Catholic Church in England.

To prevent disease occurring and to effect its cure when it has occurred, attention must, however, be paid to the laws of hygiene and sanitation. If a natural law is violated catastrophe must follow, and many will recall to mind that timely rebuke of Lord Palmerston to the Presbytery of Edinburgh when that body approached him with the request to order a national fast and day of public humiliation, in order that the cholera plague in Scotland might be stopped. The Home Secretary recommended cleansing in preference to fasting, activity to humiliation, the destruction of the causes of disease by purifying the homes of the poor, or the plague would again revisit them "in spite of all the prayers and fastings of a united but inactive nation."

Professor Tyndall's objection to prayer was only against those who used it in the belief that by its means they could bring about a contravention of natural law, "for," he said, "the latest conclusions of science are in perfect accordance with the doctrine of the Master Himself, which manifestly was that the distribution of natural phenomena is not affected by moral or religious causes," just as Mr. J. A. Hedderwick, one of the writers of the Rationalist Press Association wrote in his book, *Do We Believe?* "What is killing the belief in prayer is the evidence science has brought of the unwavering uniformity of nature, and of the hopelessly insignificant position which the world and its inhabitants occupy in the universe."

Prayer is not a force acting directly upon physical nature, nor is the order of physical nature suspended or broken in answer to prayer. Prayer cannot effect any change in the Eternal, and, if such be our object, we pray in vain. The question then may arise in our minds: "If we cannot in any way bring about this change, why pray at all?" Yet prayer is a necessity for the spiritual development of the individual, and the recognition of the truth of the unchangeableness of the Eternal is the first and most important law to be learned in what may, perhaps, be described as the art of prayer. It is the starting point, which must never be lost sight of.

To suppose that we can change Eternal Law is to assume that we are greater than the Law.

The object of prayer is not to change that which is immutable, a self-evident impossibility, but to alter the conscious or unconscious rebellion of the individual against such law or departure from it. No amount of prayer will exempt us from the working of the law of retribution.

Sir Henry Thompson; writing in the *Contemporary Review* for June 1872, said that "the value of prayer to the Deity has been recognised in all ages and by all nations," and Professor Tyndall, who took part in the discussion which was proceeding at that time, wrote: "It is not my habit to think otherwise than solemnly of the feeling which prompts prayer. It is a potency which I should like to see guided, not extinguished, devoted to practical objects instead of upon air, In some form or other, not yet evident, it may, as alleged, be necessary to man's highest culture."

What Prayer Is

RAYER IS THE COMMUNION OF the unseen self with the unseen realms; the practice of being placed in telepathic communication with minds and forces on higher planes than our own. For this words are not necessary, although they may be employed. It is by such thoughtful aspirations that we become conformable with the will of the Eternal, and prayer has for its aim the lessening of the distance between the Individual and the Eternal: not that the Supreme Power is separated from us by geographical or spatial distance. "The Eternal," said Philip Brooks, "is everywhere, giving Himself to us; the opening of the windows is a signal that we want Him, and an invitation that He will be glad enough to answer, to come into every window that is opened to Him and turned His way." We can pierce through the materiality of this expression, especially when we read the same writer's definition of prayer as "the fastening of the life on to the Eternal, the drinking of the thirsty soul of the great fountain of life," which is closely akin to that of a Swedenborgian, the Rev. James F. Buss, who said that "True, living prayer is the reaching out of the soul's hand to take the Divine blessing which the Eternal is every moment waiting to bestow."

Prayer, therefore, may be objective or subjective. When used only in an objective sense, the Eternal is invariably addressed in anthropomorphic language, and regarded as a distant resident Deity; though even in this form there have been strikingly marvellous results, as the Orphan Homes at Ashley Down, Bristol, the Quarrier Homes, and other institutions, bear witness.

M. Auguste Sabatier has pointed out that "Prayer is no vain exercise of words, no mere repetition of a sacred formula, but the movement of the soul putting itself into a personal relation of contact with the mysterious power of which it feels the presence." F. W. H. Myers has defined it as the general name for the attitude of open and earnest expectancy, and distinguishes between prayer and supplication. He

gives as the highest meaning of prayer, "communion uttered or unexpressed with the Supreme Spirit," and defines supplication as "an attempt to obtain benefits from unseen beings by an inward disposition of our own minds."

Prayer, therefore, is not a matter of petition alone, although it may sometimes take that form. It is communion with the Eternal. How tiresome we should think our little ones if they climbed upon our knees merely to ask favours; but how they gladden our hearts when the tiny hands steal around the neck and the lips utter the words, "I don't want anything, I only want to love you." That is real prayer, because it is the communion of spirit with spirit, and, as Madame Guyon has said, "Prayer is nothing but the application of the heart to God and the internal exercise of love." No further words may pass, but the communion, far from ceasing, becomes intensified, until, perhaps, the little one falls asleep in that loving, clinging attitude. The main function of prayer lies in the spiritual reign of fellowship or communion with the Eternal, as expressed by Thomas Moore in the words:

As down in the sunless retreats of the ocean
   Sweet flowers are springing no mortal can see,
So deep in the soul the still prayer of devotion,
   Unheard by the world, rises silent to Thee.

A liturgy, or any form of words, though intended as a material aid to spiritual communion, often retards it and causes the mind to centre upon the form, and thus prevents the true aspirations of the soul. This is the Buddhistic objection to prayer, for the Buddhist maintains that rituals have no efficacy; prayers

are vain repetitions; and incantations have no saving power. Prayer, for the Buddhist, takes the form of contemplation, self-examination, concentration, and aspiration.

Are liturgies or set forms of any value? We find a well-known ethical writer, Mr. W. M. Salter, saying that "Almost everyone who has tried the experiment of setting aside a little time each day for serious thought, knows how difficult it is to concentrate one's attention without some external help"; and, on the other side, a well-known Spiritualist, Mr. W. J. Colville, says; "Whoever in the calm, restful silence of a sequestered retreat can realise the highest spiritual communion with that omnipresent, Divine life, which is both Over-soul and in-dwelling spirit, needs no outward aid to devotion, and therefore can well afford to dispense with all religious and other ceremonials."

Words are not necessary or essential for prayer, which has been aptly described as

The soul's sincere desire,
    Uttered or unexpressed;
The burden of a hidden fire
    That trembles in the breast.

But when words are employed, they should be the accurate expressions of inward aspirations and not mere random utterances.

My words fly up, my thoughts remain below,
Words without thoughts never to heaven go.

said the writer of *Hamlet* (III. iii. 97).

The efficacy of Mantras lies not so much in the words themselves as in the concentration of thought expressed in the formulae. Spoken prayer is, in a sense, an incantation, and it is only when spoken by the heart as well that it has power to attract good, and repel bad, influences.

The Pharisee prayed and the publican prayed, but the utterances of the first-named were characterised by the "official polish" which is a feature of most liturgical prayers, and bore upon the face of it evidence of rehearsal in private before being publicly uttered. The prayer of the publican was a cry wrung from the heart. It was spontaneous, not formal, and its spontaneity ensured its answer. Liturgies or set forms were unknown to the early Christians, and are a relic of pagan customs.

One of the requisites of prayer is our consciousness of the deep necessity of that for
which we pray or desire and the possibility of
our receiving it. Mrs. Besant, in her work on
Thought Power, said: "The frequent effectiveness of prayer over ordinary good wishes is due
to the greater concentration and intensity
thrown by the pious believer into his prayer.
Similar concentration and intensity would

bring about similar results without the use of prayer."

But to pray only, without putting forth effort, is useless. A student about to sit for an examination will do well to pray and keep his mind firmly centred upon success, but, at the same time, he will find it advantageous and even necessary to master the contents of the prescribed text-books. The wisdom of Cromwell's advice to "Trust in God and keep your powder dry," cannot be questioned. True prayer will lead to labour, to the putting forth by the individual of the effort to fall into line with and accomplish the will of the Eternal when that will becomes known as the result of prayer and meditation. That will be an exercise of zeal in the right direction. Paul, as a Pharisee, was zealous, but his zeal was misdirected.

We want to realise the serious importance of prayer. We want to pray and not to babble. A few seconds on our knees, with the thoughts far away from the words uttered, is not prayer.

We may even be constantly in prayer without ever getting on to our knees. But whatever may be the physical attitude, let the mind be concentrated—a concentration corresponding

in degree, though not in kind, with that practised by the Fakirs in their physical austerities.

Self-deprecation is not prayer. Prayer must
be positive, a demand, even, rather than a
request, a demand springing from the consciousness that we are only asking for what is
ours by right of attainment. Prayer—not saying
prayers—is intense concentration, in consequence of which there is a strong outflow of
magnetism into the ether, of thought force
which pervades the ether surrounding the individual. "He who thinks prays," said the Count-
ess of Caithness in *The Mystery of the Ages*,
"and one who disdains the spiritual exercises
of St. Ignatius may respect the transcendental
exercises of the Platonists."

By continuance in prayer we make our religion what the very word signifies it should be—
a matter of daily living. "Sacrifice," says Mr.
Gorham in his *Ethics of the Great Religions*,
"is religion made easy," but when religion
becomes bound up with life, it is not so simple
as when it is confined to observance on one day
of the week with occasional holy days added,
when attendance at some public ceremony or
function is regarded as discharging all the
obligations. When religion springs from an

internal source and does not become perverted with theological dogmas which cramp the intellect, there is little necessity to set up an external code of laws or commandments for the regulation of conduct, which will then become self-regulating.

It is the conscious, constant intimacy with what Emerson described the Oversoul; the Buddha, the Uncreate; the Jews, the Eternal; the Moslem, Allah; and the Christian, God. There must be such perfect and complete harmony between the human desire and the Divine Will as to ensure that the human desire will be granted.

Prayer is not the condescension of the Eternal to the human, but rather the ascension of the human towards union with the Eternal.

Buddhism rejects prayer, yet there is no religion that more completely emphasises the true meaning of prayer. It is a complete and perfect system of meditation and concentration, and that is prayer.

A number of clergymen once waited upon President Lincoln, and in the course of the interview expressed the hope that God was on their side. Mr. Lincoln replied that he wished to make sure that he was on God's side. Prayer is the harmonising of the self with God, the constant aspiration towards the Ideal, and is, or should be, realised in the constant progressive character of the individual. It should not be a personal petition for a personal favour. "Seek ye the kingdom and all these things shall be added unto you." Prayer is the seeking of the kingdom, "the kingdom is within you," and it is the most effective aid to self-realisation.

Men are sometimes apt to think that the mere act of prayer will lead to the imparting of some divine or holy influence to them. Such thoughts have a tendency to cause prayer to become a mere formality and to lack the necessary concentration. It is well "always to pray and faint not"; yet prayer must be spontaneous, the outcome of a continuous process, a constant state of watchfulness combined with prayer.

A most forceful article on Prayer appeared in *The Kalpaka*, an Indian monthly magazine, for July 1910, from the pen of Mr. A. P. Mukerji, from which I cull the following extract: "Prayer is the concentration of the spirit on the problems of the Divine Life; the turning of the search-light of the superconscious self upon the riddles of existence. Prayer is the filling of inner

vision with positive light—light that rends
asunder the veils of Darkness and Maya. Prayer
is the soul-ascent up the magnetic chain of Evolution. Prayer is the meditation on the Infinite
in the silence. Prayer is the faith of the seer in
his vision; in his contemplation of the facts of
life, inner and outer, subjective and objective,
from the highest standpoint; in the utmost trust

that he reposes in the Infinite Law, that sweetly and steadfastly seeks to ever provide our feet with iron shoes for rough roads."

Prayer, true prayer, should never be limited to petition, even if, indeed, it takes that form at all. There are other factors which must enter into it—contemplation, examination, meditation, realisation of the unseen—and the individual should cease from active and conscious prayer only to enter into the state of non-conscious dependence upon the Unseen and thus continue in prayer, although the conversation and thoughts have perforce to be in another direction.

If what is frequently called "the pattern prayer" or "the Lord's Prayer" is carefully examined, it will be seen to consist of affirmations and not petitions, and, moreover, that these affirmations are of a spiritual and not a material character. The only "petition," strictly so-called, "Give us this day our daily bread," should, in the opinion of more than one commentator, be translated "May we remain content with our daily lot."

If, however, prayer does take the form of petition it must be offered with the intention of securing the accomplishment of Divine purposes by the employment of Divine methods. It should be confined to spiritual necessities. "Your heavenly Father knoweth that ye have need of these things (food and raiment). But seek ye first the kingdom of God and his righteousness; and all these things shall be added unto you."

THE EFFECT OF PRAYER
UPON CHARACTER

 RAYER CANNOT IN ANY WAY EFFECT A change in the Unchangeable or alter the Immutable. The effect produced is not upon the Eternal to Whom our prayers are addressed, but upon the pray-er, the one that prays, and our prayers meet with the response harmonising with the plane to which we have attained. Thus St. James in his Epistle (v. 16) lays emphasis upon the value of the prayer of a righteous or just man, and gives an example by recalling the acts of Elias. It may, therefore, be truly and reverently said that we answer our own prayers. This truth was emphasised by Maximus of Tyre, when he said, "He that prays either is worthy of the things he prays for, or he is not. If he is, he will obtain them, though he prays not, and if he is not, he will not obtain them, even though he prays." Every idea is fulfilled as soon as it is conceived. "What things soever ye desire, when ye pray, believe that ye receive them and ye shall have them." Jesus Himself carried out this thought in the miracle of the multiplication of the loaves and fishes: He prayed, blessed and gave thanks, and then distributed the food to the multitude.

The effect of prayer upon the individual has received scientific corroboration, for the art of photography has revealed the beautiful, clear light rays which emanate from the person engaged in prayerful meditation, and help us to understand the symbolism of the narrative in which we read of the veil with which Moses had to cover his face after communion with the Eternal. The late Dr. Baraduc, the eminent nerve-specialist of Paris, demonstrated that intense prayer expresses itself in a shape like a tongue of fire; and Dr. J. M. Peebles, in one of his works, says that by arrangement with half a dozen devout persons, a prayer meeting was held in an apartment at the top of the Eiffel Tower. The special camera was arranged in position, and, at a given moment, Dr. Baraduc took the picture. "The result was a very clear and impressive representation of the thoughts and aspirations of those intensely earnest souls, rising like a column of incense as though

ascending direct to the very throne of God."
This gives demonstration that the joy which
many experience after seasons of prayer has
some solid foundation, It is said of Walden,
Abbot of Montrose, that when in darkness and
agony, he would, in anguish of soul, cast himself upon the ground and pray with the utmost

earnestness. He no sooner rose from his prayer when he found the thick mist of darkness which had overwhelmed his mind scattered and his soul suddenly filled with light, fervour, and an inexpressibly holy joy, in which he sang the praises of divine mercy with an interior jubilation which seemed to give him in some degree a foretaste of the joys of the blessed.

Henry Wood has defined scientific prayer as "getting into accord with the Universal Good," and adds that "Formal words are but the shell of true prayer, which is as necessary for the spiritual selfhood as breathing to the lungs." Another of our modern writers, Miss Lilian Whiting, has given expression to the same thought in the following words: "Through prayer, the absolute communion with the Divine, we may live in constantly increasing receptivity to the divine forces." If we recognise this principle as an axiom, we can appreciate the spirituality of the prayer of Sophocles:

"Oh, that my lot might lead me in the path of holy innocence of thought and deed, the path which august laws ordain, which in the highest heaven had their birth, neither did the race of mortal men beget them, nor shall oblivion ever put them to sleep: the power of God is mighty in them, and groweth not old."

In sentiment this is akin to a prayer of King Alfred the Great, which has been preserved to us in the records of English literature:

"Guide me to do Thy will, to the needs of my soul, better than I can myself. And steadfast my mind toward Thy will, and to my soul's need. And strengthen me against the temptations of the devil, and put far from me my foul lust and every unrighteousness. And shield me against my foes, seen and unseen. And teach me to do Thy will, that I may inwardly live before Thee, before all things with a clean mind and a clean body."

Each of these prayers falls into line with the statement of Matthew Arnold in *Literature and Dogma*. "All good and beneficial prayer is, in truth, however men may describe it, nothing else than an energy of aspiration towards the Eternal Not-Ourselves that makes for righteousness, of aspiration towards it and co-operation with it. Nothing, therefore, can be more efficacious, more right, and more real."

Madame Guyon recommended meditative reading as a step towards meditation *pur et simple* and meditative prayer, discarding the frequent repetitions of set forms or studied prayers. The final step in her *Method of Prayer* is also the attainment of Divine Union, a state analogous to Nirvana, in its true meaning, for, as she describes it, it is the destruction of self. The path is a solitary one, and the utmost a teacher can do is to show the pupil the path and then let him walk alone. Her words remind one forcibly of the well-known Buddhistic lines:

> We ourselves must walk the path—
> Buddhas only teach the way.

The value of prayer in the formation of character is set forth in the words of Jesus (Matthew vi. 44): "I say unto you, love your enemies; bless them that curse you; do good to them that hate you; and pray for them that despitefully use you and persecute you." There is a gradation in these four precepts. The first or highest is that of exhibiting love for those we should generally class as our enemies, a condition of mind more difficult of attainment than the blessing of those that curse us; which, in its turn, is not so easy as doing good to them that hate us, which might become an act performed out of pure philanthropy. What is regarded as the easiest task of all is to pray for them that despitefully use and persecute us— one of the petitions in what is known as the Lord's Prayer. If, from our hearts, we put this last precept into practice, the higher steps will not be so difficult of ascension. Thus prayer will gradually assume its highest form and become the sincere uplifting of the soul to the Source of all power, with the burning desire to achieve inner wisdom. And what Jesus taught, the Gospel records tell us, He put into practice. When upon the cross, reviled by his persecutors, the human nature sank in order that the divine might gain the ascendancy, and the cry rose to heaven, "Father, forgive them, for they know not what they do."

Mr. W. P. Swainson says that the leading idea of Boehme was "life, prayer being the means whereby the soul soars above the *centrum naturea*, the abyss of hell, and the spirit of this world, and penetrates into the Light, into Christ, into the Heart of God. In true prayer will and desire are one." This spiritual communion is necessary for the true development of character, and was recognised by Thomas Carlyle in *Past and Present*: "He who takes not counsel of the Unseen and Silent, from him will never come real visibility and speech"; and again in *Hero Worship* "Can a man's soul, to this hour, get guidance by any other method than intrinsically by that same devout prostration of the earnest, struggling soul before the Highest, the Giver of all Light; be such a prayer a spoken, articulate, or be it a voiceless, inarticulate one? There is no other method."

The man of prayer will not want to advertise the fact; he will not often, if at all, be seen in the act of prayer, but the result of his praying habit will be seen by his power of attracting good and repelling bad influences. Constantine was known as a man who said many prayers because he gave instructions for his likeness to be stamped upon the gold coinage representing him in the act of prayer, and this money became current throughout the Roman world. Nearly all the paintings of him also gave the impression that he was constantly engaged in conversation with God. True prayer will, however, lead to humility.

There was a remarkable change depicted in the attitude of Jesus consequent upon the three prayers in the garden recorded in Matthew xxvi.

Before the prayer He said (verse 38), "My soul is exceeding sorrowful, even unto death." Then He left them, and in the anguish of sorrow "fell on His face, and prayed, saying, O my Father, if it be possible, let this cup pass from me!" May we not imagine that there was a break in the prayer before the next sentence was uttered, a heart struggle between inclination and duty, with a victory for duty, and then came the next and final sentence of that prayer, not, perhaps, without a sob—"nevertheless, not as I will, but as Thou wilt"? There was, however, the immediate as well as the future duty, and so He rose and went to the sleeping disciples. Back again to prayer. But the tenor of the utterance had changed; there was the added note of resignation to a Higher Power, always the result of true prayer, "uttered or unexpressed": "O my Father, if this cup may not pass from me, except I drink it, Thy will be done." The prayer had been answered. But those disciples are sleeping. They do not seem to realise what is about to happen. They, too, must be awakened, for they have to watch—and pray, and so He journeys forth again to waken them. But we do not read that this time they were awakened, and Jesus, maybe, hurried back to spend another season of prayer and communion with the Eternal to make sure and steadfast His resignation to the Divine Will. There was no occasion for any alteration in the prayer: the human will had fallen into line and tune with the Infinite, and so "He went away again, and prayed the third time, *saying the same words.*" First conflict, then resignation, and then strengthening, and we seem to be able to detect a ring of joy, a thrill of exultation, a gladsome surrender, as the command broke forth upon the night air to those heavy-eyed, wearied disciples, "Rise, let us be going." Before prayer He fell on His face; now after prayer He arose and went forth to love and duty. It was all the outcome of prayer, and what was possible for Jesus is possible for everyone.

The whole scene is so intensely human that we lose immediately the beauty of it when we postulate omnipotence and omniscience for Jesus.

His attitude at the first prayer betokened selfishness, albeit the selfishness was of a more refined character than generally displayed. That selfishness disappeared during the prayer,

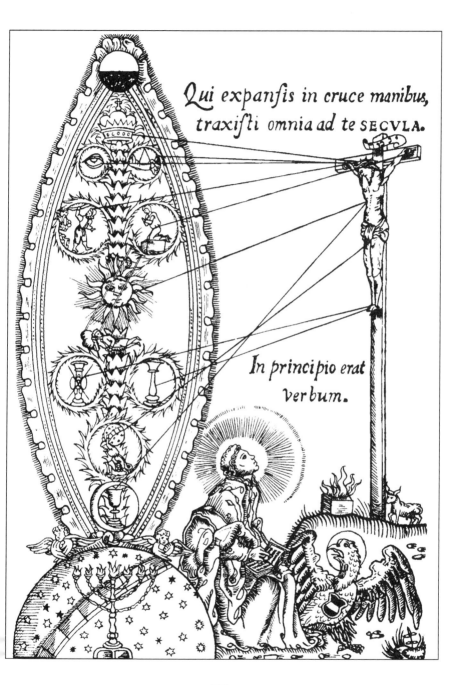

Qui expanfis in cruce manibus,
traxifti omnia ad te SECVLA.

In principio erat
verbum.

and we notice the ascendancy of the Christ—
that Christ life which will do and die for others.

Prayer purifies desire, and thus, if in no
other way, results in advantage and profit to the
individual. It develops his sympathy and leads
to the conquest of selfishness. The desire
becomes cleansed from all unrighteousness,
and the individual is led away from the valleys
of sin, soars above the mountains of selfishness,
leaves dogmas and creeds behind, together with
fear, sorrow, and suffering, and ascends into
the realities and enjoys a communion which is
untranslatable into ordinary, common, everyday speech. We may begin with words, but
words soon fail us; we may set out with the
intention of "approaching the throne of grace,"
but we end in blissful, indescribable, unemo-
tional communion with the power behind the
throne, for we have discovered "the secret place
of the Most High."

As we gaze upon your glory,
Saints of God, in Heaven's own light,
Teach us how we too may join you,
How to win-those crowns so bright.

Would you come where we have entered?
Fight with all your strength and power;
Would you live the life eternal?
Die to self at every hour,

Ah! we shrink from pain and sorrow,
We are frightened when we hear
We must live in constant struggles,
We must die to all that's dear.

If the path be rough and thorny,
At the end all pains shall cease;
If the battle be a fierce one,
There shall be eternal peace.

Catholic Hymn.

Bibliography

Arnold, Matthew. *Literature and Dogma*. London: Smith, Elder & Co., 1883.

Bellarmine, Cardinal Robert. *Spiritual Writings*. Mahwah, NJ: Paulist Press, 1989.

Besant, Annie. *Thought Power: Its Control and Culture*. London: Theosophical, 1920.

Budge, Sir E. A. Wallis, trans. *The Book of the Dead*. London: British Museum, 1899.

Carlyle, Thomas. *Hero Worship*. London: Chapman & Hall, 1888.

——. *Past and Present*. London: Oxford University Press, 1909.

Colvill, Helen Hester. *Saint Teresa of Spain*. London: Methuen, 1909.

Demosthenes. *De Corona*. B. Drake, ed. London: MacMillan, 1928.

Draper, John William. *History of the Conflict between Religion and Science*. London: Kegan Paul, Trench, Trubner, 1896.

Erasmus, Desiderius. *Praise of Folly*. Betty Radice, trans. New York: Viking Penguin, 1971.

Farnell, L. R. *The Evolution of Religion: An Anthropological Study*. London: Williams & Norgate, 1905.

Gorham, Charles T. *Ethics of the Great Religions*. London: Watts, 1904.

Guyon, Madame Jeanne-Marie Bouvier de la Motte. *A Short and Easy Method of Prayer*. Reprint, London: Hodder and Stoughton, 1990.

Hamman, Adalbert, ed. *Early Christian Prayers*. Chicago: Franciscan Herald Press, 1961.

Harrison, Jane. *Prolegomena*. London: Meridian Books, 1963.

—. *Themis*. London: Merlin Press, 1963.

Hastings, James. *Encyclopaedia of Religion & Ethics,* Vol. X. Edinburgh: T & T Clark, 1918.

Hedderwick, J. A. *Do We Believe?* In *The Creed of Christendom: Its Foundations Contrasted with Its Superstructure*. London: Watts, 1905.

Homer. *The Iliad*. London: John Wiley & Sons, 1999.

Hooke, S. H. *Babylonian & Assyrian Religion*. Oxford: Basil Blackwell, 1962.

Hormusji, Byramji. "Andambar, the Indian Lourdes." In *Annals of Psychical Science,* June-July 1908.

Langdon, Stephen. *The Mythology of All Races: Semitic Mythology*. Boston: Rowman and Littlefield, 1931.

MacKenna, Stephen and B. S. Page, trans., *Plotinus: The Six Enneads*. Chicago: Encyclopedia Britannica, 1952.

Mangin, M. Marcel. *The Lourdes Cures and Metapsychical Science. Annals of Psychical Science*. February 1908.

Mead, G.R.S. *Echoes from the Gnosis,* vol. VI: A Mithraic Ritual. London: Theosophical Society, 1907.

More, Thomas. *Utopia*. Spingfield, IL: Templegate, 1999.

Mukerji, A. P. Article in *The Kalpaka*. July 1910.

Myers, F. W. H. *Human Personality and Its Survival of Bodily Death*. Reprint edition, Charlottesville, VA: Hampton Roads, 2001.

Oldfather, C. H. *Diodorus of Sicily,* vol. 1. London: William Heinemann, 1933.

Osuna, Francisco de. *Tercer Abecedario*. In print as *Francisco de Osuna: Third Spiritual Alphabet*. Mary Giles, trans. Mahwah, NJ: Paulist Press, 1982.

Rig Veda. Wendy Doniger O'Flaherty, trans. London: Penguin, 1981.

Shakespeare, William. *Hamlet*. Washington Square Press, 2003.

Spiritual Exercises of St. Ignatius of Loyola. W. H. Longridge, trans. London: Robert Scott, 1922.

Taylor, Thomas. *The Eleusinian & Bacchic Mysteries*. New York: J. W. Bouton, 1875.

Tyrrell, Father George. *Lex Orandi, or Prayer and Creed*. London: Longmans, 1904.

Wallace, Alfred Russel. *On Miracles and Modern Spiritualism*. Reprint edition, London: Routledge, 2001.

Yonge, C. D. *The Works of Philo*. Peabody, MA: Hendrickson, 1993.

INDEX

hypostases, 35–36
Hyslop, Theodore B., 87
Ignatian prayer, 75
Islam, 63; prayer in, 67–68
Jesus, 84, 114, 118, 119;
  prayer in the garden,
  120–124
Leo X, 4
Lesser Mysteries, 37
Leucippus, 4, 58
Lex Orandi, 76
Lincoln, Abraham, 107
Literature and Dogma, 117
liturgy, 101
Lodge, Sir Oliver, 85
Lord's Prayer, 16, 17, 110, 119
Lourdes Cures and Metaphysical Science, The, 87–88
Luther, 90
man of dust, 25
Mangin, M. Marcel, 87, 88
Manichean religion, 66
mantras, 103
materialism, 2–3, 4, 58
Maximus of Tyre, 113
meditation, 72
meditative reading, 117–118
Melanchthon, 90
mental prayer, 71
Method of Prayer, 118
Michael of Coutances, 75
Mind Cure, Faith Cure and the Miracles of Lourdes, 88
Miracles and Modern Spiritualism, 84
Mirandola, Pico della, 4
Mithraic Mysteries, 38
Mithraic Prayer of Invocation, 39–41
Mithraism, 38
Mithras, 38
monasteries of fourth century, 43
Moody, D.L., 93

Moore, Thomas, 100
More, Thomas, 3, 58
Morning Prayer, A, 18
Moses, 30, 59
Mukerji, A. P., 108
Myers, A. T., 88
Myers, F.W.H., 80, 88, 98
Mystery of the Ages, 106
Mystery Schools, 37
Mystical Theology, The, 44
natural law, 93–96
Nicholas of Cusa, 4
Nicholas V, 4
nirvana, 118
On the Vision of God, 34–35
One, The, 35
Origen, 66
Orpheus, 18, 27, 30, 32
Osiris, 80
Osuna, 71
Palmerston, Lord, 93–96
Past and Present, 119
Pater Noster, 16
Peebles, J. M., 114
Pentateuch, 12
petition, 100, 110
Pius II, 4
Plato, 32, 64
Plotinus, 32, 34–35, 36, 37;
  teaching of hypostases,
  35–36
prayer, as an art, 27, 49–51;
  aspirational, 73; prayer to
  Bel, 10–11; as bribery, 63; in
  Buddhism, 101–102, 107;
  and character, formation of,
  118; cleaving to will of God,
  73; as communing with God,
  24, 47–48; cures in non-
  Christian traditions, 88–92;
  to the dead, 79–80; and disease, 87–94; effect of, indirect, 52–53, scientific
  corroboration of, 114–115;